UNDERSTANDING
CORMAC
McCARTHY

Understanding Contemporary American Literature
Matthew J. Bruccoli, Series Editor

Volumes on

Edward Albee • Sherman Alexie • Nicholson Baker • John Barth
Donald Barthelme • The Beats • Thomas Berger
The Black Mountain Poets • Robert Bly • T. C. Boyle • Raymond Carver
Fred Chappell • Chicano Literature • Contemporary American Drama
Contemporary American Horror Fiction
Contemporary American Literary Theory
Contemporary American Science Fiction, 1926–1970
Contemporary American Science Fiction, 1970–2000
Contemporary Chicana Literature • Robert Coover • James Dickey
E. L. Doctorow • Rita Dove • John Gardner • George Garrett
John Hawkes • Joseph Heller • Lillian Hellman • Beth Henley
John Irving • Randall Jarrell • Charles Johnson • Adrienne Kennedy
William Kennedy • Jack Kerouac • Jamaica Kincaid
Tony Kushner • Ursula K. Le Guin • Denise Levertov
Bernard Malamud • Bobbie Ann Mason • Cormac McCarthy
Jill McCorkle • Carson McCullers • W. S. Merwin • Arthur Miller
Lorrie Moore • Toni Morrison's Fiction • Vladimir Nabokov
Gloria Naylor • Joyce Carol Oates • Tim O'Brien • Flannery O'Connor
Cynthia Ozick • Walker Percy • Katherine Anne Porter
Richard Powers • Reynolds Price • Annie Proulx
Thomas Pynchon • Theodore Roethke • Philip Roth
May Sarton • Hubert Selby, Jr. • Mary Lee Settle • Neil Simon
Isaac Bashevis Singer • Jane Smiley • Gary Snyder
William Stafford • Anne Tyler • Kurt Vonnegut
David Foster Wallace • Robert Penn Warren • James Welch
Eudora Welty • Tennessee Williams • August Wilson • Charles Wright

UNDERSTANDING
CORMAC
McCARTHY

Steven Frye

The University of South Carolina Press

Published by the University of South Carolina Press
Columbia, South Carolina 29208

www.sc.edu/uscpress

Manufactured in the United States of America

18 17 16 15 14 13 12 11 10   10 9 8 7 6 5 4 3 2

Library of Congress Cataloging-in-Publication Data

Frye, Steven.
    Understanding Cormac McCarthy / Steven Frye.
        p. cm. — (Understanding contemporary American literature)
    Includes bibliographical references and index.
    ISBN 978-1-57003-839-6 (cloth : alk. paper)
    1. McCarthy, Cormac, 1933– —Criticism and interpretation.
  2. Southern States—In literature. 3. West (U.S.)—In literature.
  4. Mexican-American Border Region—In literature. I. Title.
    PS3563.C337Z66 2009
    813'.54—dc22

                                                                2009009376

For Kristin, Melissa, and Thomas with love

Contents

Series Editor's Preface

The volumes of *Understanding Contemporary American Literature* have been planned as guides or companions for students as well as good nonacademic readers. The editor and publisher perceive a need for these volumes because much of the influential contemporary literature makes special demands. Uninitiated readers encounter difficulty in approaching works that depart from the traditional forms and techniques of prose and poetry. Literature relies on conventions, but the conventions keep evolving; new writers form their own conventions—which in time may become familiar. Put simply, *UCAL* provides instruction in how to read certain contemporary writers—identifying and explicating their material, themes, use of language, point of view, structures, symbolism, and responses to experience.

The word *understanding* in the titles was deliberately chosen. Many willing readers lack an adequate understanding of how contemporary literature works; that is, what the author is attempting to express and the means by which it is conveyed. Although the criticism and analysis in the series have been aimed at a level of general accessibility, these introductory volumes are meant to be applied in conjunction with the works they cover. They do not provide a substitute for the works and authors they introduce, but rather prepare the reader for more profitable literary experiences.

M. J. B.

Acknowledgments

This book explores the fiction of an author who has spent much of his adult life writing in relative obscurity, often with the support of faithful editors and generous grants and fellowships, but for the most part out of the public eye. Before the accolades that came with his later works, many of his novels were out of print. Over those many years, the author showed little concern over this, becoming perhaps without knowing it an archetype of artistic focus and intensity. The personal motives for this reaction find their origin in the recesses of an individual personality, and I have no desire to speculate on the behavior of a living author who in recent years has emerged as one of the most important novelists of the late twentieth and early twenty-first centuries. The best focus is the works themselves, and now that the later ones have thrust him into public view, the whole of his canon exists in reprint editions that can be found in any major bookstore. Like many academic readers, I came to McCarthy with *Blood Meridian* and the Border Trilogy, motivated by a twin interest in the American romance and the literature of the American West. But in my evolution as a McCarthy scholar, I have studied and written on the southern novels and the dramatic works and have found in them a rich variety in theme, style, and intellectual interest. I have my favorites, those works I think stand apart, as well as those I consider less meritorious. My sentiments and perspectives might perhaps be gleaned from these pages, but I have done my best to limit them, to give each novel its due, and to bear in mind that "understanding" a work does not mandate a general assessment of its value in comparison to

others. Judgments of this sort are always subject to reconsideration, are sometimes motivated by an ill-conceived academic hubris, and are perhaps best relegated to hallway conversation or the always enjoyable coffeehouse book chat. This is a teaching volume, and I have attempted to provide a thorough treatment of influence, formal aesthetics, thematic texture, and historical context—those things that give students and thoughtful readers a sense of an author's purpose and emphasis. In this endeavor I have drawn from the support of many colleagues, fellow McCarthy scholars, as well as friends and family.

I would like to thank my friend and colleague Eric Carl Link, professor and chair of the English department at the University of Memphis. Eric and I have worked together for over fifteen years, first as graduate students at Purdue University, then on a series of articles and an edited collection, and finally as coeditors of an academic journal. He has read this book in various draft forms, and his remarkable blend of incisive criticism, judgment, and unstinting faith has been invaluable. Thanks go as well to my longtime friend Greg Trine, a creative writer working outside the academic field, who helped me by providing the fresh perspective of the thoughtful nonacademic reader. I would also like to thank Jerome Klinkowitz, editor of the *Norton Anthology of American Literature,* volume E, for his insightful reading and careful line editing, as well as Edwin T. Arnold for his careful reading and commentary. Over the years, I have gained immeasurably from my association with many McCarthy scholars, a number of them active members of the Cormac McCarthy Society. These include Dianne C. Luce, Rick Wallach, David Cremean, Christopher D. Campbell, Stacey Peebles, Nick Monk, Jay Ellis, Susan Hawkins, John Wegner, John Cant, and my own student Alan Noble. The selected bibliography that concludes

this volume owes much to Dianne C. Luce's online bibliography on the Cormac McCarthy Society Web site. My study of the tradition of the American romance, especially in the nineteenth century, has been enriched over the years by G. R. Thompson, Robert Paul Lamb, and the late Cheryl Oreovitz, as well as Derek Parker Royal, an eminent Philip Roth scholar who recommended that I propose this volume. I have also benefited much from the perspective of thoughtful McCarthy aficionados outside the academic realm who read portions of this book and kept me mindful of audience. These include Greg Young, Michael Young, and Bryan Young. Thanks also to my colleagues in the English department at California State University, Bakersfield, for their support and encouragement, and to the professional staff at the CSUB Walter Stiern Memorial Library, especially Kristine Holloway and Jamie Jacks. A special thank you to my parents, Ed and Joann Frye, whose support and attention have been unwavering, flowing always from a wellspring of selflessness. And as always, my deepest appreciation goes to my wife of nearly twenty years, Kristin, whose mind and heart are as strong as they are tender, and who enriches all that I do. Finally, thanks to my children, Melissa and Thomas, who daily take me away from the densities and darkness of McCarthy's world and remind me that innocence and wisdom blend beautifully in simple harmony.

UNDERSTANDING
CORMAC
McCARTHY

Understanding Cormac McCarthy

Early in his writing life, Cormac McCarthy renovated a dairy barn as a living space, salvaging bricks from the boyhood home of James Agee. In building a new house from old stones, he was mirroring practice that would define his writing for the next forty years. In an interview dealing primarily with *Blood Meridian,* Harold Bloom argues that the novel is defined by "a surge of narrative propulsiveness . . . an astonishing charge of language, which, finally, in spite of its clear Faulknerian and Melvillean affinities and sources, goes back . . . to *their* source . . . Shakespeare."[1] In his many works, McCarthy selectively dismantles and reconfigures the great landmarks of literary art—the King James Bible, Shakespeare's tragedies, the novels of Melville, Dostoyevsky, Faulkner, and Hemingway—and out of the shards and raw material he makes something distinctively his own. McCarthy's early novels are set or at least drawn from experiences in his home state of Tennessee, often in the rural regions of the Appalachian Mountains near Knoxville, but they always occupy a nameless landscape rich in image and symbol, rendered in evocative and lyrical prose. This mythic quality made his transition to the West a natural one, and many readers encountered his work for the first time with his best-selling novel *All the Pretty Horses,* which won the National Book Award in 1992. In many ways his novels and plays are uniquely American, and their nationality is marked by the narrative forms and thematic

preoccupations typical of the American romance. His enigmatic characters are real and supremely human; yet they are richly symbolic as well. He is an energetic literary stylist who explores a host of themes rooted in a diverse array of philosophical perspectives. As an author concerned with the formal nature of his art, he participates, in dynamic retrospective, in the tradition of Western world literature from its beginnings to its late manifestations in the twentieth century.

Life and Career

Charles Joseph McCarthy, Jr., the son of Joseph McCarthy and Gladys McGrail McCarthy, was born in Providence, Rhode Island, in 1933 and raised in Knoxville, Tennessee, where he was first exposed to the people and the places that would occupy his southern works. He later took the name "Cormac" (the Gaelic equivalent of Charles), which was a family nickname given to his father by his Irish aunts. McCarthy was raised a Roman Catholic and was educated in Catholic schools until he entered the University of Tennessee in 1951. He was always active intellectually, though in his early years he was not necessarily bookish. Still, when asked by his grammar school teacher if he had any interests, he discovered that "I was the only one with any hobbies, and I had every hobby there was."[2] But reading and writing were not initially among them, and it was only later—after leaving the university in 1953 for the U.S. Air Force and being stationed in Alaska—that he discovered books, primarily as a way to indulge his varied intellectual interests and mollify the tedium in the barracks. He returned briefly to the University of Tennessee in 1957. He soon discovered his literary talents, later winning the university's Ingram-Merrill Award for creative writing. Two of his short stories, "Wake for Susan" (1959) and

"A Drowning Incident" (1960), were published in the school's literary magazine, the *Phoenix*. He left the university without taking a degree to begin work on his first novel, *The Orchard Keeper*, which was ultimately published by Random House in 1965 under the guidance of Albert Erskine, William Faulkner's editor.

Although they sold only sparsely, McCarthy's early novels generally received positive reviews. Eschewing a conventional working life, he dedicated himself to the Spartan simplicity he felt was necessary in order to devote himself fully to writing. As a young man, he married twice, having one son with his first wife. For two decades he survived primarily on awards earned for his early novels, including grants from the Rockefeller Foundation, the William Faulkner Foundation, the American Academy of Arts and Letters, and later the Guggenheim Foundation. Throughout his career he remained private, rejecting lucrative offers for speaking engagements. In 1976 he moved from Tennessee to El Paso, Texas. He was awarded the MacArthur Fellowship in 1981, and he later married Jennifer Winkley and moved to Santa Fe, New Mexico, as a fellow at the Santa Fe Institute, working primarily among scientists, both writing and exploring a range of interests at least partly outside the intellectual mainstream, including, among other things, chaos and complexity theory. Described by Robert Coles of the *New Yorker* as a novelist of religious feeling, McCarthy in all his works engages the ultimate questions—the nature of the real, the possibility of the divine, the source of ethics and identity—but always in a richly philosophical context and with an active interest in secular science.[3] In his midsixties he became the father of John Francis McCarthy, to whom his Pulitzer Prize–winning novel, *The Road*, is dedicated.

Overview: Influence and Innovation

In coming to terms with Cormac McCarthy's works, readers face two principal challenges. First, McCarthy sometimes employs narrative techniques that are unconventional, involving frames, inversions, digressions, dream sequences, and extended interior or exterior monologues. One must explore how these various layers integrate or remain purposefully distinct. McCarthy, then, must be approached aesthetically, always with an eye toward the themes implied in literary form. His narrative textures mirror the mysteries of the natural world. The three interwoven stories in *The Crossing,* spoken at length by characters, suggest a metaphysical source and an underlying order in nature, which he renders in detailed description. The dream monologue that concludes *Cities of the Plain* implies the complexities of the unconscious and the role of beauty in providing a compensatory order to the chaos of human perception. The formal features of each of McCarthy's works must therefore be charted and explored, and he becomes genuinely distinctive in the context of individual sentences, which are characterized by a unique voice, a lyrical and descriptive style, and a vocabulary rife with uncommon and often archaic words. In a rendering of the nighttime world surrounding Judge Holden in *Blood Meridian,* he describes that world as "some vortex in that waste apposite to which man's transit and his reckonings alike lay abrogate. As if beyond will or fate, he and his beasts and his trappings moved both in card and in substance under consignment to some third and other destiny" (96). His purpose here is to emphasize the power of language to treat philosophical ideas poetically, to heighten the reader's sense of the primordial mystery in nature, and to explore the complex ways human lives are bound with others. First and foremost then, coming to terms with McCarthy's

works requires close and dedicated attention to the intricacies of form, as well as to the complexities of language, style, and voice. Individual passages must be read, reread, and pondered, always with a playful acceptance of their ambiguity.

The second challenge is simpler yet perhaps more formidable. All the author's works, especially *Outer Dark, Child of God, Blood Meridian,* and *The Road,* deal directly with violence, human degradation, and both human and natural evil. These are some of McCarthy's primary concerns, and he more than confronts darkness—he seeks its deepest recesses. In Herman Melville's terms he is "a man who dives." While many readers are immediately drawn to the intensity of McCarthy's prose, others find the subject matter tremendously difficult to absorb. One must come to understand that McCarthy, though reclusive, has given clues as to his evolving worldview. Though in brief interviews he expresses uncertainty about the answers to essential questions—the existence of God, the relationship of good and evil, the nature of transcendent moral purpose and order—McCarthy is by no means devoid of hope. On the contrary, if genuine hope is to be found by honest and thoughtful people, it must be found by acknowledging the harshest realities and the darkest of human circumstances.[4] In *Suttree* the sordid social outcasts face degrading physical and economic conditions, but they find meaning in the sense of community they form among themselves. In *The Road* the prospect of cosmic annihilation must be seen alongside the touching intimacy of the father and the son, and one must consider the possibility that "goodness" and "luck" may in the end preside. In his only television interview, McCarthy was asked what he wanted his readers to take away from *The Road.* His answer: "That we should be grateful." When reading even the most disturbing of McCarthy's

works, one must understand that the author seeks truth and value. Sometimes these things prove elusive, but always he leaves readers with beautiful, sometimes incomparably evocative prose. The concluding paragraph of *All the Pretty Horses* stands as one of many examples: "He touched the horse with his heels and rode on. He rode with the sun coppering his face and the red wind blowing out of the west across the evening land and the small desert birds flew chittering among the dry bracken and horse and rider and horse passed on and their long shadows passed in tandem like the shadow of a single being. Passed and paled into the darkening land, the world to come."

In his most extended print interview, "McCarthy's Venomous Fiction," which was conducted by Richard B. Woodward of the *New York Times Magazine,* McCarthy discusses the role of influence in the creation of new works of literature. He says, "The ugly fact is books are made out of books. . . . The novel depends for its life on the novels that have been written."[5] Woodward gives a sense of McCarthy's mind, his voracious appetite for an eclectic range of interests—scientific, philosophical, and literary—from Mojave rattlesnakes with neurotoxic venom, to Gnostic cosmology and chaos theory, to the intricate narrative structures of the American romance. The author is unapologetic in acknowledging his literary forebears, prizing specifically Melville, Dostoyevsky, and Faulkner, and expressing some distaste for Marcel Proust and Henry James. He takes in the past, its forms, preoccupations, and language, but his own work is infused with the historical weight of the twentieth century—the traumatic social transformation of the American South in the postbellum period, the human carnage of two world wars and the genocidal waste that attended them, as well as the

angst that emerges from the development of the technological and nuclear age.

McCarthy's telling comment in the Woodward interview can be illuminated by considering T. S. Eliot's "Tradition and the Individual Talent" (1920). Eliot suggests that literary history is dynamic, and the contemporary writer actively participates in the tradition that precedes him. It is certainly true that authors read, are profoundly moved and inspired, and out of that experience, they create. McCarthy is very much this "traditional" author in the terms Eliot articulates. He evokes the past in all its forms and connotations, and he "builds" his works out of a life-long reading practice that absorbs and reenvisions, apprehends and recontextualizes. Critics both popular and academic have noted echoes of Homer and Dante in McCarthy's works, as well as the lyrical cadences of the King James Bible and Shakespeare, but the tradition he engages most directly involves the American romance, from its inception in James Fenimore Cooper and William Gilmore Simms, to its later and more complex manifestations in Melville and Hawthorne, and finally to the postbellum modern romances rooted in the South, primarily the works of his immediate predecessors William Faulkner, Erskine Caldwell, Carson McCullers, and Flannery O'Connor. Thus he can be understood in part in the context of literary history, as an author who works with, at the very least, three forms and movements: the frontier romance; the philosophically preoccupied yet ambiguous narratives of Melville, Hawthorne, Poe, and Dostoyevsky; and the tradition of the southern gothic and the southern grotesque. In all his works McCarthy is concerned with the human drama in all its facets, the forces of history, and with the role of violence in the life of the world writ large. Again, in

the Woodward interview, he says, "There is no such thing as life without bloodshed. . . . I think the notion that the species can be improved some way, that everyone could live in harmony, is a really dangerous idea." For all his fascination with science, which continued at the Santa Fe Institute, he is no positivist, no vanguard supporter of eighteenth-century Enlightenment notions of human perfectibility. Violence is a reality endemic to the world's existence; depravity and avarice are central to human nature; and meaning, purpose, and value, if they are to be found, must be sought in darkness. These themes pervade his work, and they are central to his unique contribution to the development of the American novel, which is marked by his distinctive integration of style, language, and a rich array of compelling philosophical and religious perspectives.

McCarthy's reconfiguration of the frontier romance can be seen in the southern works as early as *The Orchard Keeper* and in the western works as late as *Cities of the Plain* and *No Country for Old Men.* In America this genre harkens back to the early nineteenth century, in John Filson's "nonfictional" accounts of Daniel Boone, the revolutionary war novels of William Gilmore Simms, and, most notably perhaps, the *Leatherstocking Tales* of James Fenimore Cooper. Central to these works were mythology and the mythic hero. Characters were created to embody human traits but were larger than life, emblematic of a culture's values, aspirations, ambitions, and self-perceptions. In early American epic romances, the mythic hero finds himself a player in a sweeping drama that pits the forces of historical progress—the settlement of the frontier by European civilization—against the forces of reaction, which involves the attempts made by Native Americans and white frontiersmen to preserve older and simpler ways of living. Thus the inevitability, the mixed benefit, and even the

tragedy of these events emerge as central concerns. McCarthy's works can be understood as "revisionist" frontier romances, but one must take care in defining this term. *The Orchard Keeper, Child of God, Blood Meridian,* and the novels of the Border Trilogy are not overtly political; yet they are often rooted in the historical concerns of the twentieth and twenty-first centuries. The forces of civilization are by no means portrayed in a celebratory light, as industrial technology, American business interests such as Texas oil, even the building of the interstate highway system, often leave the hero displaced and bereft of purpose. Incidents of greed and malevolence abound, as scalp hunting, drug running, even nuclear apocalypse, all find their way into McCarthy's epic vision. But the forces of reaction—those players in the drama who stand against the new order—are by no means ethically pure. The issue of morality stands in the foreground of these novels, but the precise pathway to right action is never easily charted.

The wilderness is of course the setting of the frontier romance, and many McCarthy novels take the American landscape, often in its roughest yet most pristine form, as not only setting but subject, as a context through which the human impulse to physical brutality may be explored. In rural Tennessee in the 1930s, *The Orchard Keeper*'s John Wesley Rattner takes Arthur Ownby as a mentor, and from him he learns the principles of self-reliance, a code of individualistic heroic action founded upon a preindustrial dependence on the land. But these lessons lose their value as each man faces modernity—specifically the political power of the Tennessee Valley Authority—and as Ownby ends up in that darkest and most humiliating of all modern mazes—a mental institution. *Blood Meridian* and the Border Trilogy evoke the conventions of the frontier most

directly, at least most recognizably. Set in the West, they are journey novels, coming-of age stories involving young heroes seeking
identity and a sense of place. *Blood Meridian* is unflinching in its
"revisionist" account of the darker realities of westward expansion, as the Glanton Gang begins with a legal mandate to take
scalps and assist in quelling the alien land. But any attempt to
read the novel as a single-minded political allegory revealing the
avaricious impulses of Manifest Destiny is undermined by the
character of the judge. He is a ubiquitous figure who transcends
race, nationality, or political purpose, and he becomes many
things, among them, the richly symbolic incarnation of "mindless violence," a propensity that lies latent even in the kid, in
spite of his stoic resistance. *All the Pretty Horses,* the first novel
in the Border Trilogy and McCarthy's most popular novel until
The Road, involves a momentary softening of perspective, and
the story's appeal lies in part from a stark beauty of description
and a sense of nostalgia often characteristic of the frontier
romance and the western genre. But even here, the central subject is the violence present in the human heart, as the hero John
Grady Cole kills another young man in self-defense, fights his
impulse to take brutal revenge on a cruel Mexican captain, and
seeks moral exoneration and secular absolution from a kind and
benevolent judge in his home state of Texas. This softening is less
prevalent in the second two novels of the trilogy, both of which
remain rooted in the western genre and the frontier romance, but
engage philosophical issues recontextualized and deeply
ensconced in the historical settings of the twentieth century—in
brothels, on decaying ranches and rancheros, along highways
with blood-red sunsets perhaps brought on by the nuclear tests
in the American Southwest. For McCarthy, the frontier romance
in all its historical scope is simply, or not so simply, a means to

explore the human potential for violence, avarice, blindness, self-gratification, and depravity. The author infuses the genre with a philosophical content, using what begins as a popular form to enrich his characters both psychologically and ethically. Protagonists such as John Wesley Rattner, the kid, John Grady Cole, and Billy Parham, each engage in a personal quest, but with a pressing moral urgency.

McCarthy has often been characterized as a philosophical and even religious writer in the broadest, most eclectic, and unorthodox sense. Academic critics have observed the echo of worldviews ranging from Platonism, Neoplatonism, the Existential Christianity of Søren Kierkegaard, Gnosticism, Nietzschean materialism, to the mystical and heterodox Christianity of Jakob Böhme. The metaphorical and symbolic systems McCarthy employs suggest ancient Judaism, and the elements of the divine found in his novels, which are always represented suggestively rather than definitively, imply Yahweh the lawgiver, the Gnostic demiurge (the evil force that governs the material world in Gnostic philosophy), and Elohim (the benevolent fertile crescent God who appears first in the Old Testament and achieves full expression in the incarnation of the Father in Christ). The paradoxical range of perspectives McCarthy explores, sometimes in a single work, suggests not confusion but instead his rich and complex set of formal and thematic concerns. Works such as *Blood Meridian, The Road,* and *The Sunset Limited* systematically position characters in order to permit contentious interaction, as they deal with the deepest and most vexing questions. Judge Holden in *Blood Meridian* has been compared to Dostoyevsky's Grand Inquisitor in *The Brothers Karamazov,* specifically in his antipathy to any concept of human decency. He stands in contrast to the kid, who clings however tenuously to a faith in the

generative effect of moral action and benevolence. In *The Sunset Limited,* a street preacher by the name of Black debates a suicidal, atheistic college professor on the existence of God, the possibility of finding purpose in self-sacrifice, and the reality of love. For McCarthy, perhaps unlike Dostoyevsky (who tends to resolve his complex narratives within a Christian framework), these questions must be asked, pondered, articulated, recast, and provisionally explored. But they are never fully resolved, and the final word that concludes *The Road* expresses the human condition as McCarthy sees it—physically, spiritually, and intellectually. That word is *mystery*.

It is this emphasis on the unanswerable that draws McCarthy to another subgenre of the novel that dominates in American literature from the early nineteenth century forward. There is no generally accepted name for this form, though it is clearly a category of the romance. Its major practitioners are Hawthorne, Melville, Poe, and later Faulkner. One can associate many of their works with the high gothic romance in the ambiguous mode, involving novels and short stories that explore densely psychological, metaphysical, and religious issues, always with an emphasis on a darkness that implies not pessimism but radical skepticism, the notion that there are boundaries to the human intellect, realms beyond which the human mind cannot travel. This engagement with darkness as mystery explains in vivid terms McCarthy's affinity for the romance genre and for Herman Melville. In his contemporary context, McCarthy is more forthright and aggressive as he intensifies his renderings of death, fear of cosmic annihilation, and even the confusion that emerges from the diversity of the twentieth-century intellectual climate. His works seek this darkness and foreground mystery, not necessarily with any presupposition of nihilism or emptiness, but in

an attempt to engage actively in a modern context the human dilemma in its most distressing and challenging manifestations. The sometimes unconventional nature of McCarthy's narrative structures is one method for enacting this process. In novels such as *The Orchard Keeper, Outer Dark, The Crossing, Cities of the Plain,* and *No Country for Old Men,* he uses multiple interlaced strands, frames, and evocative dream sequences to unsettle the reader's faith in a distinctly perceivable world. Circumstances both interior and exterior to character are seen from many viewpoints, and there is often the mysterious, omniscient McCarthy persona that intercedes in strange, lyrical, and sometimes italicized passages to complicate and lend ambiguity to the most tactile and visual situations. The narrative intricacy can be seen in *Blood Meridian* in the distinct perspectives of three characters. In extended monologues, the judge espouses the malevolence that defines his own heart. In the middle stands the former priest Tobin, who encourages violence in the service of survival. In contrast to both is the kid, who resists the seeming omnipotence of evil in an attempt to retain his soul through guarded, albeit limited acts of service and self-sacrifice. This cosmic evil is prefigured earlier in *Outer Dark*'s mysterious triune, the three figures that follow Culla Holme, seeing into his heart and exceeding it in a cruelty and malevolence that seem beyond space and time. In all these works, McCarthy employs both character and literary form in the service of a complex of ambitious themes, all of which attempt to explore human nature under the stress of instinct, impulse, and the external forces of time and historical change.

Especially in the initial reviews of his early novels, McCarthy has been associated with the regional literature of the South. Again, McCarthy shares an affinity with William Faulkner, Erskine Caldwell, Tennessee Williams, Flannery O'Connor, Carson

McCullers, and Walker Percy, among many others. These authors are distinctive both thematically and formally, since they explore the historical conditions of the South following the Civil War, as well as the traumatic psychological and social circumstances that became more acute in the modern period. Central to the evolving aesthetics of southern literature is the southern gothic and the southern grotesque.[6] Speaking to a group of librarians at the University of Virginia in 1936, Ellen Glasgow coined the term "southern gothic" to describe what she saw as a disturbing feature of the new southern writers, specifically Caldwell and Faulkner. These authors employ many of the conventions of the gothic romance—decaying edifices, bleak settings, psychologically tortured protagonists—and place them in recognizably southern settings. In part, the purpose is to evoke both terror and horror, to externalize the emotional distress that attends social transformation, and to connote the perversity inherent in human nature. Tennessee Williams once described the southern gothic as "an intuition, of an underlying dreadfulness in modern experience."[7] Ancillary to this genre is the southern grotesque, which involves obscene and often comic exaggerations in character and situation, sometimes involving physical deformity and sexual deviance.

In emphasizing the theme of mystery, McCarthy certainly draws from this southern tradition. In *The Orchard Keeper,* the murder of John Wesley's father is made horrific yet comic as the body is guarded in the orchard by Uncle Ather. There is an irony in Arthur Ownby's ignorance of the corpse's identity and in the fact that the young man unknowingly befriends the murderer. In *Outer Dark* the evil embodied in the grisly triune is strangely justified by Culla Holme's incest and the abandonment of

his infant child. In *Child of God* the southern grotesque takes center stage as the necrophiliac Lester Ballard—after losing his land—precipitously descends into a psychological abyss, into realms of cruelty and perversion unimaginable. In a distinctively southern style, McCarthy explores the absurdity of certain social conventions and the basic weakness and fallibility of human nature.

To understand and come to terms with Cormac McCarthy's novels and plays, one must engage the intricacies of each individual work—the narrative layers, the linguistic complexity, the erudite vocabulary, even the profound nature of his philosophical themes. This task is made less formidable for readers as they understand the manner in which he creatively reenvisions the traditions that precede him, most notably the frontier romance, the densely philosophical and ambiguous romances of the nineteenth century, and the literature of the American South in the postbellum period.

McCarthy's passion for the life of the mind is palpable, and his eclectic interests often find their way into his works. Thematically, he is varied, difficult to pin down, often changing philosophical masks within a single work. But even here one may map at least part of the terrain. The ethics and metaphysics of Judaism and Christianity, the Gnosticism of the Ancient Near East, and the more modern considerations of Böhme, Hegel, Kierkegaard, and Nietzsche, are all ideas he chooses to consider, and in many cases he integrates them into coherent if complex character configurations that stand alone as literary creations, ultimately independent of influence. In the end, however, McCarthy's works should be approached with the simple anticipation of beauty, for in each case readers experience an avalanche

of words, images, and richly embodied landscapes and characters. Equipped with some grasp of aesthetic form, tradition, and the history of ideas, readers may come to a satisfying understanding of this important contemporary author.

The Southern Works

In 1957, after two years stationed in Alaska with the U.S. Air Force, where he spent much of his spare time reading, McCarthy returned to Knoxville to continue his degree in liberal arts. He was in every sense returning home, to the burgeoning southern city where he had lived since he was four years old. His father moved the family there in 1937 to take a position as a lawyer with the Tennessee Valley Authority, the public improvement agency responsible for many of the physical and social changes that transformed the rural mountain region in the early twentieth century. Even the most cursory reading of McCarthy's southern works reveals the importance of place in the author's conception. The manners, language, values, even the most basic perceptions of characters such as Arthur Ownby, John Wesley Rattner, Culla Holme, and Cornelius Suttree are imbued with the shapes and shades of the darkening land, as well as the strangeness, the oblique sense of gray, fatalistic, mystical apprehension that distinguished many Appalachian people since their first migration from northern Britain, southern Scotland, and Ulster Plantation. After his return to Knoxville, McCarthy's active but varied intellectual interests seemed to coalesce in the ambition to write. While at the University of Tennessee, he published two stories, "Wake for Susan" and "A Drowning Incident" in the *Phoenix,* a student literary magazine, both under the name "C. J. McCarthy." In later years he would playfully distance himself from these early forays into southern landscape

and character. He turned down the opportunity to have them reprinted in the *Virginia Quarterly* and said that he hoped to be long in the grave before they surfaced again. This sensitivity emerges perhaps from the observable fact that McCarthy's literary sensibilities changed with *The Orchard Keeper,* since this novel involves a greater intensity of lyrical expression as well as a complex interweaving of narrative strands reminiscent of Faulkner and other high modernists. Still "A Drowning Incident" and "Wake for Susan" provide a glimpse into the author's skill with language and his preoccupation with the defining influence of region on the interior landscape of the human mind. Tellingly "Wake for Susan" begins with a quote from Sir Walter Scott, suggesting perhaps an emerging interest in the historical romance. In appealing if somewhat sentimental terms, the story recounts the experience of a young man named Wes, who on a hunting trip happens upon a gravestone wrapped in vines, sinking into the moist earth. It is the grave of a young woman with the inscribed date 1834, and Wes conjures the outward struggles and inward details of the girl's first experience with love. The story takes time as its subject and in a prose replete with natural description attempts to universalize the girl's short life, as Wes creates a more complete story from the fabric of his own imagination, one that the gravestone only dimly suggests. The prose is refined if somewhat conventional, suggesting the author's interest in nature, human isolation, and loss. "A Drowning Incident" tells the tale of a boy who recovers the drowned body of a puppy that has been cast into the Tennessee River. The sketch concludes in grotesque fashion as the boy, motivated by thinly repressed rage, places the dead puppy in a crib next to the sleeping form of his infant sibling. Like "Wake for Susan," this story evokes a rural setting but in a fashion darker and more indicative of the

novels that will follow—rich in description but with a stark more naturalistic rendering of setting and circumstance. Both prose pieces are comparatively well crafted, if somewhat immature in comparison to later works, but together they provide a view into McCarthy's emerging style and thematic interests. At least indirectly, they anticipate the concerns of the four novels of the Tennessee period, works that deal with nature, history, social change, and the omnipresent reality of mystery and the unknown, especially as it confronts the intensities of human consciousness and perception. Though his southern novels were published between 1965 and 1979, he returns to the South in later years with *The Road,* and rural Appalachia and its environs form the setting for his screenplay, *The Gardener's Son,* a historical drama based on actual events dealing with two nineteenth-century South Carolina families, directed by Richard Pearce in 1976 for the PBS "Visions" series. *The Stonemason,* a play written previously and published in 1994, deals with many of the central themes of the southern novels: the value of intimacy in the context of family heritage, as well as the mystical experience that characterizes the work of the traditional craftsman, who understands that "true masonry is not held together by cement but by gravity . . . by the warp of the world" (9).[1]

The Orchard Keeper (1965)

Written after the author left the University of Tennessee, in part while he was working at an auto-parts store in Chicago, *The Orchard Keeper* is more experimental than many of his later works, if not thematically at least formally. Initial reviews were generally quite positive. In the *Saturday Review,* Granville Hicks praises McCarthy's language, saying he "describes the land with precision, eloquence, and affection."[2] In the *Kirkus Reviews,*

Gabriel Chevallier responds with a tone of curiosity, claiming that the novel, "while desolate, is effective in many ways" since there is "some unusual writing furrowed by stark, visual imagery while the story itself has a shadowed fascination."[3] In *Harper's*, Katherine Gauss Jackson expresses sympathy for the formal challenges of the story, characterizing it as "a complicated and evocative exposition of the transiency of life, well worth the concentration it demands."[4] Many critics note the influence of southern literature, some suggesting that McCarthy's first effort lacked originality of design and style. An anonymous reviewer in the *Times Literary Supplement* states that "Mr. McCarthy's debt is obvious and specific: it is to Faulkner," and though the critic acknowledges the power of McCarthy's descriptive language, he concludes that the author "gives the impression of having it in him to write a much better novel than this; but he will not do so while he confuses his Tennessee with [Faulkner's] Yoknapatawpha County."[5] Other reviews relish what they see as the freshness of McCarthy's narrative voice. In the *New York Herald Tribune Book Week*, James R. Frakes views the novel as "Trim but not skeletal, poetic but not effusive . . . a refreshing and rewarding accomplishment."[6]

McCarthy's first extended effort received respectable if not considerable attention, and critics recognized elements of originality as well as the author's participation in a rich and varied American tradition. In its overt mythology and preoccupation with the effects of historical change on individual lives, as well as its vivid descriptions of nature and the land, the novel draws from the conventions of the American historical romance. Set in the rural regions around Knoxville, Tennessee, between the two world wars, *The Orchard Keeper* celebrates in romantic terms the rejuvenating power of nature and the values of simple living,

and out of this affirmation criticizes the sometimes destructive forces of industrial civilization, implicitly embodied in the various improvement projects of the Tennessee Valley Authority. In this regard, the novel reflects the essential values of the Southern Agrarians, an eclectic group of authors, poets, and scholars who emerged in the 1930s, many of them working out of Vanderbilt University in Nashville. They include Robert Penn Warren, John Crowe Ransom, Allen Tate, and Richard M. Weaver. These writers were at times associated with a conservative politics, though many of them, most notably Robert Penn Warren and John Crowe Ransom, later distanced themselves from the more extreme political implications of Agrarian reactionary sensibilities. Essentially, they were concerned with the negative effects of the industrial capitalism and urbanization that characterized the modern period, advocating with varying degrees of intensity a return to traditional, agricultural, even rural modes of living and social organization. At a thematic level, the primary conflict in *The Orchard Keeper* is between the forces of historical progress and reaction, as the aging woodsman Arthur Ownby, known as Uncle Ather, stands guard over an apple orchard and the decaying corpse of Kenneth Rattner. Unaware of the identity of the body, he serves as mentor to the dead man's son, John Wesley Rattner, who from an early age has sworn to avenge his father's murder. At intervals in a complicated plot, both Uncle Ather and John Wesley encounter the outlaw and bootlegger Marion Sylder, who many years before had killed Kenneth Rattner in self-defense, although John Wesley doesn't know it. Sylder assists the boy in various ways, at one point defending him against a corrupt sheriff's deputy, and their lives become intertwined in a web of circumstances that none of them can control or understand. Uncle Ather's desire to remain close to the primal and

redemptive forces of nature, his efforts to help John Wesley learn the lessons of the land, stand in conflict with the social and economic changes of the twentieth century, embodied physically in the towns, cities, highways, and bridges that perpetually intrude upon their lives. In all this, through a series of extended and lyrically rendered descriptions, nature becomes a character, a truly dynamic presence within the novel. Though the three men encounter one another, their stories are told separately in distinct story strands, and McCarthy resists the temptation to unify them through any formal devices. As such, the novel's experimental quality becomes evident in a triple plot made more complex by extended descriptions and interlaced strands of memory that break the temporal sequence of the story.

Coming to terms with the narrative complexity of *The Orchard Keeper* requires a close attention to these various narrative lines. Shifts in point of view, typically from John Wesley Rattner, to Uncle Ather, to Marion Sylder, are usually marked by chapters and sometimes by section breaks between paragraphs. Point of view is consistently third-person limited omniscient; though again, the linear flow of time is often broken by the extended reflections in memory clearly identified in italics. Within these various narrative strands, which can be linked to specific characters, the omniscient narrator sometimes intercedes in renderings of setting more often than not designed to blend the "character" of nature with the lives of the men involved in the story. In fact, the novel begins with an abstracted vignette in italics, as three unnamed men struggle to break apart a tree stump only to find a wire fence grown into it, thus introducing at the onset one of the novel's essential themes, the perpetual struggle between nature and civilization, industrial modernity and the primitive land.[7]

The novel is divided into four parts, with each character's perspective woven into each, and the jarring effect of these shifts in point of view is mitigated only by considering the thematic result. As their individual lives intersect, each man remains bound in the isolation of his own consciousness, his own interior world. This emphasis on human isolation appears as each character responds to present experience by remembering the past. Though he appears only briefly before his death, in part 1 Kenneth Rattner walks into a tavern and what he sees inspires an extended recollection of the Green Fly Inn near Red Branch, the small community where the major events of the novel take place (incidentally recalling the Red Branch Cycle in Celtic mythology). In part 2, as Uncle Ather stands looking over the apple orchard and the iconic water tank that intrudes upon the land, he remembers the day he discovered Kenneth Rattner's body, having been told of its whereabouts by two frightened children. A particularly extended memory sequence begins and nearly ends the third chapter in part 2, in which John Wesley Rattner recalls capturing a sparrow hawk and claiming a bounty after the bird dies. This passage anticipates a later event, when after gaining a greater respect for the land and the values embodied in Uncle Ather, he tries to reclaim the dead hawk and return the bounty. These descriptive memory strands become interior tales within larger stories told from distinct perspectives. Each discrete point of view runs parallel with the other, and though the characters interact, their tales remain largely separate. Here McCarthy pioneers a narrative technique he uses often in his later novels, a technique that, in spite of the similarities noted by critics, distinguishes him from William Faulkner. While Faulkner breaks time sequence in extensive monologues written in streams of consciousness, he usually does so by rendering

the actual thoughts of the people in his imaginary world. Mc-Carthy employs an objective narrator that tells the story from the visual and sensory perspective of characters, without fully entering their minds, thus preserving a sense of mystery, as individuals react in unknowable ways to an irreducibly complex world. In *The Orchard Keeper,* these narrative elements are integrated thematically by nature and natural imagery and by the central tension between the land and the industrial forces that attempt to contain and control it.

It is through this essentially historical conflict that McCarthy elevates Uncle Ather and John Wesley Rattner to the level of myth and draws from the tradition of the American historical romance. In one sense, the novel is contemporary to McCarthy's time, since it is set during his childhood and only thirty years from the present. Historical novels are more often set in periods distinctly remote from the author's own. But in Uncle Ather, McCarthy is preoccupied with the past, and the primary concerns that interest writers of American historical novels are central to *The Orchard Keeper.* An important feature of the historical romance, from its beginnings in the novels of Sir Walter Scott, to James Fenimore Cooper's *Leatherstocking Tales,* to many of William Faulkner's works (in this case most notably *Go Down, Moses*), is the mythic hero, and in American literature this hero often finds his home on the frontier.[8] Uncle Ather is the iconic representative of an old order, a time when survival, human happiness, even spiritual sustenance came from cultivating a synergistic relationship with the untamed wilderness. Except during brief intervals, the old man avoids the town, living in an old cabin in the mountains. Like a sentinel guarding the gateway to another world, he presides over the orchard, at various moments recalling a time when his interaction with the

savage land was deeper and more fulfilling. He stands caught in the cataclysmic sweep of time, and he is an emblem of a previous age that must inevitably give way to the inexorable forces of the modern world.[9]

The tragedy of his circumstances is dramatically captured as he wistfully and playfully recalls earlier years when panthers (or "painters") freely prowled the woods at night, strange avatars from another world, in their mystery and power evoking fear and reverence. There is a mystical quality associated with the animal (which anticipates the author's later treatment of the wolf in *The Crossing*), and one may observe echoes of the transcendentalist nature worship of Ralph Waldo Emerson and Henry David Thoreau. But Uncle Ather's perception of the spirit of nature is darker and more mysterious, consistent with a form of fatalism common among many Appalachian mountain people. At the deepest psychological and spiritual levels, the panther both attracts and repels. As John Wesley and a group of young men sit and listen, Uncle Ather tells the quasi-mythological ghost story of his attempt to hunt a marauding panther: "'You see,' he said slowly, darkly, 'they's painters and they's painters. Some of em is jest that, and then there's others is right uncommon. That old she-painter, she never left a track. She wadn't no common kind of painter'" (157). Though there is a playfulness in the old woodsman's retelling, for him the "uncommon" and mysterious become incarnate in the physical world when it is uncorrupted by industry, and right living comes from understanding and participating in a humble interaction with these primordial forces. Uncle Ather becomes the mythic personification of this recognition, representing a system of values that defined the old order and the frontier experience. He feels his association with the past but also his sense of displacement, when coming out of the

mountain he encounters a man-made pit of burning cedar. There he experiences "the old fierce pull of blood in power and despair, the pulse drum of the irrevocable act. . . . On his face a suggestion of joy, of anguish—something primitive and half hidden" (158). The old man is recognizably similar to the aging Natty Bumppo in James Fenimore Cooper's *The Prairie* and to Uncle Ike McCaslin in Faulkner's "The Bear." As the mythic hero of the American frontier, his purpose is to experience, live, and teach, and his student is John Wesley, who learns from the old man and changes as a result, becoming more adapted to the land and its power, as is exemplified by his thwarted attempt to return the bounty for the sparrow hawk. But tragically the young man recognizes that the past and the present are incommensurate, since all that remain of the frontier after Uncle Ather is captured and confined are the vague shadow figures of "myth, legend, dust" (246).

These essentially reactionary and even romantic themes, which extol the mystical qualities of the natural world, are orchestrated through beautiful and lyrically rendered descriptions. These passages involve "nature" narrowly construed as an uncorrupted but shrinking wilderness, but they are also descriptions of setting broadly. Some of the most pleasurable features of McCarthy's writing might be these sequences. In *The Orchard Keeper,* McCarthy initiates a notable feature of his emerging style, the selective placement of obscure, specialized, or archaic words, which serve the purpose of heightening the mysteries of the natural world. Words such as "carapaced" (*OED:* "the upper body-shell of tortoises, and of crustaceans"), "saurians" (*OED:* an adjectival form for "an order of reptiles"), and "parthenogenesis" (*OED:* "asexual reproduction, as by fission or budding") are known to some readers but are unrecognizable

to most, and language itself becomes a means of foregrounding the unknowable, embodied in even the most physical and tactile of human experiences. The impenetrable complexities of human consciousness appear in the deliberately elusive manipulation of style, word choice, and sentence structure, as when Uncle Ather works his way among the trails, eluding the pursuit of the sheriff. He sees and contemplates something as simple as the shattered rocks of a quarry: "the tiered and graceless monoliths of rock, alienated up out of the earth and blasted into ponderous symmetry, leaning, their fluted faces pale and recumbent among the trees, like old temple ruins" (189). A vocal minority of critics have objected to the complexity of passages such as this, but their purpose is to alter the perception of the reader, to take commonplace images and render them uncommonly, and to lend them a kind of religious and mystical quality.

These quasi-religious images are intimately bound with the tendency to portray nature through the use of allusion and symbol. The panther (in other places in the novel appearing in Uncle Ather's repeated dreams of "Cats") and the sparrow hawk, who looks at John Wesley, "*eyeing him without malice or fear—something hard there, implacable and ungiving*" (77), are examples of compelling symbols with an array of suggested meanings. But more extended descriptions invite even deeper contemplation, as nature becomes more than natural history, but a dark window that glimpses the mesmerizing landscape of another world: "The old man kept to his course, over last year's leaves slick with water, hopping and dancing wildly among the maelstrom of riotous greenery like some rain sprite, burned out of the near-darkness in antic configuration against the quick bloom of the lightning" (172). Nature becomes a primordial language of oblique suggestion, rife with elusive meanings that transcend the

material and scientific, and physical description is metaphorical and deeply rooted in literary tradition. Particularly notable in this regard is the carnivalesque imagery used when John Wesley enters Knoxville and sees the parade, with the tuba player "*red-faced and wild*" and buses spewing "*balls of hazy blue smoke*," the entire city of "*bare outlandish buildings . . . adorned with fantastic motley; arches, lintels, fluted and arabesque*" (80–81). This use of the carnivalesque suggests the boundaries of knowability, the omnipresence of mystery, and a vague sense of the perverse and decadent. Rich and conflicted representations of the natural world appear also in *The Orchard Keeper* in McCarthy's liberal use of the sublime, specifically when Uncle Ather witnesses a storm: "And the wind rising and gone colder until the trees bent as if borne forward on some violent acceleration of the earth's turning and then that too ceased and with a clatter and hiss out of the still air a plague of ice" (171). Beauty in this and other passages involves a pairing of opposites, as the natural and sensually pleasing phenomena of wind and the earth's rotation, together with "trees" and "ice," are combined with the unsettling violence and disorder that vaguely connotes a metaphysical cause, all this being typical of the sublime images in other works of Western literature. Broadly construed then, *The Orchard Keeper* emphasizes the transformative power of nature, employing language, allusion, and symbol that are elsewhere in the novel combined with biblical allusion, nightmare fantasy, and dream memory, among other descriptive devices. Taken together, they place the characters in a world of mystery. Uncle Ather, John Wesley Rattner, Marion Sylder, even nature itself become bound together in an incomprehensible play of historical and cosmological forces, in a bittersweet novel that celebrates the past even as it passes into memory.

Outer Dark (1968)

McCarthy's second novel takes its name from Matthew 8:10–12, when Christ speaks to a centurion who has come to ask for his servant to be healed. The centurion, a man outside the Hebraic "kingdom," humbles himself, and Jesus takes the opportunity to admonish those who presume themselves chosen: "Verily I say unto you, I have not found so great faith, no, not in Israel. And I say unto you, That many shall come from the east and the west, and shall sit down with Abraham, and Isaac, and Jacob, in the kingdom of heaven. But the children of the kingdom shall be cast out into the outer darkness: there shall be weeping and gnashing of teeth." In a novel set in a nameless southern locale, with only brief clues as to the story's historical context, McCarthy broadens the biblical motifs in a parable simultaneously mythic and symbolic, universal in theme, but distinctively real in its evocation of the natural world, dialect, regional manners, and social texture. But for McCarthy, at its heart, "outer darkness" is to a large extent the absolute condition of the human experience.

A young man named Culla Holme has fathered his sister's child. Telling her the infant has died, he abandons the helpless baby boy in the forest. It is recovered by an itinerant tinker whom Culla has rebuffed and is soon given to a wet nurse. Discovering the deception, the mother, Rinthy, sets out to find her child. What follows is a quest novel that shifts from journey to journey, each punctuated by interlaced vignettes recounting the horrific exploits of a murderous band of outlaws, the mysterious "triune" who seem the agents of Fate or Necessity itself. In guilt and shame, Culla wanders in the "outer dark," and from the inception a bleak determinism defines the evolving circumstances that impel him into deeper realms of choiceless despair. *Outer Dark* is a novel that draws clearly from the traditions of

the southern gothic and the southern grotesque, but in its displacement from time, its biblical resonance, and its use of the quest motif, it seeks to place in the foreground the universal themes of isolation and loss, the consequences of sin, and the possibility of redemption amid decay and degradation. Through the triune and the figure of the blind man (who appears in the final chapter), the novel marks McCarthy's entry into Melvillean romance, as it explores the force and limitations of human agency in a vast and mysterious universe, as well as the potential role of the divine in shaping human destiny.

Initial reviews of *Outer Dark* were quite varied, many of them laudatory but few of them indifferent. Critics again noted the influence of Faulkner. In the *New York Times*, referring to the rural environment, the details of the setting, and the quest, Thomas Lask suggests that the story has a "Faulknerian profile."[10] In the *New Yorker*, reminding readers of McCarthy's success in winning the William Faulkner Foundation Award for *The Orchard Keeper*, Robert Coles writes: "'Light in August' comes to mind as 'Outer Dark' unfolds: the poor white people, the harsh Puritanism, the disastrous collision of Instinct with Piety and Custom, and the imagery—of the exiles, the wanderers, the outcasts, all dressed up, though, in rural American habit."[11] But like many reviewers of *Outer Dark*, Coles considers the novel in terms distinct from the Faulknerian influence, more so than many reviewers of *The Orchard Keeper*, and in doing so begins to anticipate McCarthy's considerable literary gifts: "Not for a long time has an American writer—a young one, at that— attempted to struggle with the Fates and with what Plato called their mother: Ananke, or Necessity."[12] Other critics were equally enthusiastic. In the *New York Times Book Review*, Guy Davenport weighs in on the somewhat contentious debate regarding

McCarthy's language and sentence complexity, arguing that, "so hard-wrought a style is not in the least precious. Such bookish diction complements the countrified one," further claiming that the author's discipline "comes not only from mastery over words but from an understanding wise enough to dare tell so dark and abysmal a story."[13]

Throughout McCarthy's career, arguments about his work seem to energize around matters of style, and the initial readers of *Outer Dark* seemed to gravitate to the question of whether the author's archaic language and elaborate syntax involved legitimate aesthetic experimentation, artistic innovation, or conversely, confusion, failure, and pretense. In the *Times Literary Supplement,* André Deutsch is moderate though critical, saying that "McCarthy has come up with a sort of sub-biblical rhetoric which tends to detract from the better things in the book."[14] But in the *Washington Post Book World,* Patrick Cruttwell is scathing and even dismissive. He notes the influence of Faulkner but calls McCarthy a "lesser" writer, claiming that he draws from Faulkner "the interminable shapeless sentence and the trail of very literary epithets which look impressive unless you are unkind enough to ask what they really mean."[15] An implicit criticism of Faulkner is imbedded in this argument, and early in the review Cruttwell calls *Outer Dark* "a piece of very, very murky Gothic horror."[16] Clearly, the shadow of Faulkner still looms large in reviews of these early novels, to varied sometimes positive and negative effects, but the comparison remains valid in the sense that both writers engaged in radical forms of experimentation, both at the level of narrative form and in the style, structure, and lexicon employed. In McCarthy's case, particularly considering *Outer Dark,* it would be a lamentable act of hagiography to assume these ventures always succeed, but it is an

equally unfortunate dismissal to deny that they are purposeful and even noble attempts to achieve something authentic and new. In the end, as the majority of critics note, his success is considerable. Cruttwell's reference to "Gothic" is telling and accurate, speaking directly to the occasional obscurity present in the author's selections of words. *Outer Dark* alternates between the colloquial and regional and the erudite and sophisticated, grounding the lives of Culla and Rinthy in the bleak social circumstances of the southern poor. As Culla travels, he encounters an old man and talks with him. The old man speaks in dialect, with the lyrical cadences of the region's language and the distinctive turn of phrase grounded firmly in place. Referring to a well, he says, "Used to be a spring back of here but it dried up or sunk under the ground or something. Sunk, I reckon. Year of the harrykin. Blowed my chimley down. Fell out of the yard and left a big hole in the side of the house" (119). Here McCarthy captures details with a carefully articulated literary slight of hand. Unlike many of the early dialect experiments of the nineteenth-century local colorists, which were often difficult to understand, the old man's speech preserves nuances of dialect even within individual words, such as "harrykin," "blowed," and "chimley," yet the passage is clear and lucid, understandable and easy to read without sacrificing authenticity. But this emphasis on place coalesces around a set of densely philosophical themes that in the end invite a more elevated literary language. In the same interchange with the old man, these issues still find expression in the colloquial. Arguing that there is an unknowable purpose to all events in nature, the old man expresses himself through a quasi-religious mysticism that finds solace in human limitations, particularly as they relate to knowledge and wisdom. He says, "The more I study a thing the more I get it backward. Study long and

ye study wrong. That's what a old rifleshooter told me oncet beat me out of half a beef in a rifleshoot. I know things I ain't never studied. I know things I ain't never even thought of" (125).

This claim may seem to express the anti-intellectualism typical of many people living within the old man's social circumstances, but taken in the broader context of the novel his thoughts reflect the author's assent to the impenetrable mystery that is always at the heart of the gothic romance at its best. The unearthly triune that trails Culla and Rinthy allude to this same mystery, and McCarthy's description of the abandoned infant displays the extremes of his experimental rhetoric, as well as an evocative sense of human isolation. Individuals must flail against the unknowable densities of a vast ungraspable universe. The child lies in the forest, a "shapeless white plasm struggling upon the rich and incunabular moss like a lank swamp hare" (17). Before the tinker sees the boy, he hears it:

> He would have taken it for some boneless cognate of his heart's dread had the child not cried.
>
> It howled execration upon the dim camarine world of its nativity wail on wail while he lay there gibbering with palsied jawhasps, his hands putting back the night like some witless paraclete beleaguered with all limbo's clamor. (17–18)

The prose has a quality of elusiveness that invites attention and scrutiny, in words such as "camarine" (*OED:* "a fetid marsh or swamp), "paraclete" (*OED:* "a title given to the Holy Spirit [or occas. Christ]: an advocate, intercessor; or a helper or comforter), as well as the more commonly understood term "limbo" (*OED:* "a region supposed to exist on the border of Hell as the abode of the just who died before Christ's coming, and of unbaptised infants"). When the meaning of these words is determined,

a different thematic dimension appears, one that in no way compromises but instead deepens the evocative religiosity of the passage. The fetid marsh implies decay, and the paraclete or comforter is now witless and abandoned, with limbo giving the reader a sense of the "outer dark" as a metaphor. It is a place where an innocent child, an everyman figure unaware of its origins, lies wailing, isolated and alone. Unlocking the meaning of these archaisms reveals a layer hitherto unseen, which involves the language of McCarthy's own Catholic upbringing, together with a heightened sense of human depravity, decadence, weakness, and susceptibility to unknown forces beyond the self. All these themes are central to the southern grotesque and the southern gothic as well as the Melvillean romance, though these genre categories by no means subsume the novel's philosophical themes, nor do they compromise its originality and distinctive voice.

In *Outer Dark* the narrative involves an integration of separate yet related stories unified by the journey motif. The chapters are untitled and unnumbered: two in third-person omniscient from Culla and Rinthy's point of view; nine in third-person omniscient from Culla's point of view; six from Rinthy's; one from the tinker's; and six italicized vignettes that separate chapters, all but one involving the triune. These journeys drive the plot, and both Culla's and Rinthy's encounters with people are quite different. As he travels, Culla looks for work and occasionally finds it, all the while meeting mysterious figures who engage him in conversations that speak, indirectly but knowingly, to his sin and plight, specifically the old man in chapter 8, the blind seer at the conclusion, and the leader of the triune. Culla's journey finds him in settings imbued with the darkness and decay typical of the gothic romance. Rinthy's world departs from this

only in the sense that she finds compassion from various people along the way, including a kind family that feeds her and a doctor who treats her because her breasts continue to produce milk. Still, brother and sister both move sightless through a wilderness of isolation and existential dread. They fly from an indefinable force embodied symbolically in the triune, a force that becomes incarnate in their own personal conflicts, in the impulses of inner gothic horror and the psychological weight of sin and guilt. The force suggested in the triune is also, in a sense, an indefinable principle of balance and justice, external to the main characters but omnipresent in the universe, which seems to demand retribution.[17]

The triune's role becomes partially clear to Culla in his first encounter with them. After an accident on a ferry, he meets them on the shore. They seem to know him and greet him with a thin veneer of hospitality, two of them gazing at him with a "predacious curiosity" (170), offering him "blackened" meat that "had the consistency of whang, was dusted with ash, tasted of sulphur" (172). The bearded man in the triune is described in strangely demonic terms: "In the upper slant of light his beard shone and his mouth was red, and his eyes were shadowed lunettes with nothing there at all" (171). The biblical allusions continue as Culla himself appears to them "like some stormy and ruinous prophet" (170). After an elusive conversation about the role of names in conferring identity on people and things, with chilling subtlety the bearded man demands that Culla give him the pair of boots he has stolen from a squire, a farmer the triune later murdered. This minor act of restitution foreshadows the novel's conclusion, and as the triune disappears into the darkness, Culla looks at the dying fire, at "a single cleft and yellow serpent tongue of flame standing among the coals" (181). In

the "outer dark," in the "camarine" "limbo" of Culla's gothic world, all he sees are the refracted symbolic outlines of his own depravity, and the avatars of Satan, the triune, are ironically the figures destined to restore a provisional balance to a world he has set askew. In the end, they do so by brutally destroying the consequences of his sin. Incest, the darkening land, the sense of dread, and the inner perversion that motivates Culla's transgression are all elements of the southern gothic as defined by Ellen Glasgow and further refined by Tennessee Williams. The setting locates the novel in the South, and the novel involves the genre conventions of many southern writers. As in the works of Faulkner, Williams, and O'Connor, there is a mythic resonance that characterizes the novel and motivates its themes.

But as Robert Coles notes, this depravity reflects the moral preoccupations of a "harsh Puritanism,"[18] and this reference is telling when considering the "Calvinistic gloom" that Melville, in praise of Nathaniel Hawthorne, associates with the "power of blackness" pervading the work of every truly great writer.[19] This interest in the consequences of human sin in a universe defined by a force shrouded in mystery is, again, configured through the triune, and their oblique purpose comes to full fruition in the end. After a compelling incident (alluding to the New Testament story) in which a group of drovers lose a herd of hogs over a cliff, Culla, having escaped them because they blame him for the accidental death of one of their comrades, finds himself sitting with the triune around a fire. The tinker who has brutally denied Rinthy the child hangs dead from a tree, a horrid grotesque destroyed by the Fates themselves, and Culla waits for the bleak and inescapable hand of retribution without fully knowing his ultimate destiny. He sees the three men, and they seem to

be "endowed with a dream's redundancy. Like revenants that reoccur in lands laid waste with fever: spectral, palpable as stone" (231). The child they now possess is described in terms of the literary grotesque: it is real and recognizable, but it is also twisted, distorted, suggesting the very perversity that brought it "wailing" into the world: "It had a healed burn all down one side of it and the skin was papery and wrinkled like an old man's" (231). As the child looks at his father Culla sees "one eyeless and angry red socket like a stokehole to a brain in flames" (231–32). The bearded man seems clairvoyant as he accuses Culla of fathering his sister's child, and Culla resists, denying the accusation as well as any concern for the boy. But his words are only a mask, since he pleads for the infant's life and tries to convince them that Rinthy will care for the child. The bearded man ponders the identity of those in hell, the idea that they have no names, and this tragically recalls the fact that in spite of Rinthy's desperate wish Culla refused to name the boy. In a brief moment that is more chilling for its understatement, the bearded man takes his knife to the child's throat. The grotesque horror of the scene, however, must be considered in the context of Culla's dramatic albeit understated transformation. The child he took from his sister and left in the woods to die, he now desperately seeks to return to her. Like Peter with Christ, he denies the child, saying, "It ain't nothing to me" (233), but his pleading for its life is measured and clear: "My sister would take him. . . . That chap. We could find her and she'd take him" (236). In this hellish scene of murder and retribution ironically defined by the demonic triune, Culla finally comes not only to understand the nature of his sin, but to desire the safety of the misbegotten child he has heartlessly abandoned. After the

murder of the boy the triune disappears, but they leave Culla alive, presumably to ponder the consequences of his actions, which he does through his encounter with the blind man.

Many years have passed, though the novel remains out of time, as Culla travels another nameless road. He encounters the sightless man, who is "ragged" and "serene," and the blind man greets him, saying he has seen him before. This wandering prophet figure treats Culla with a congeniality he has rarely encountered, and their brief conversation moves directly to the question of the divine and the nature of human destiny. Blindness appears as a telling motif that blends with the pervasive metaphor of the "outer dark," but now the darkness that shrouds the old man's vision is a darkness of inner illumination. He asks Culla if he needs anything and follows the question with the claim that he is at "the Lord's work" (240). Culla asks if he is a preacher, but the blind man responds, "No preacher. What is they to preach?" (240). The old man's serenity is clearly the outcome of the darkness that surrounds him, as he travels the road alone, offering to give what he doesn't have, concluding that all will come to him through prayer. What he sees with vivid clarity is the inexorable destiny that circumscribes every journey, and when Culla asks him why he doesn't pray back his eyes, he responds, "What needs a man to see his way when he's sent there anyhow?" (241). All that the blind man has lost is what would appear to him in the light: the blighted archetypal landscape of wilderness and decay, the "wasteland" that is in a sense the externalization of Culla's mind, the "dead land where nothing moved save windy rifts of ash that rose dolorous and died again down the blackened corridors" (242). It is here that the "outer dark" of the novel's title, so richly drawn from the book of Matthew, becomes the place where redemption becomes possible,

as Culla encounters kindness and recognition, a hand offering help from helplessness itself. This glimmer of possibility is prefigured in the same evocative religious terminology of the title, when in the previous chapter Rinthy walks among the charred ruins of the triune's camp "in a frail agony of grace" (237). The novel concludes with Culla still lost and wandering, like all human beings attuned to the mystery of their origins, but now he considers at least his obligation to help the blind man, to lead him away from the swamp he cannot see. The details of Culla's thoughts are shrouded, but in the end he displays concern, empathy, and the impulse to reach out to someone he doesn't know but instinctively recognizes as a kindred spirit. Through biblical allusions and the displacement from time, and an evocative use of character as symbol, the novel becomes a complex parable exploring the consequences of human blindness. It is a tale that portrays the way in which human actions and their consequences transform the interior "corridors" of the human soul, sometimes for the good, resonating and reverberating finally in realms beyond knowing.

Child of God (1974)

In his third novel, McCarthy evokes realms of human degradation striking and rare even in the works of contemporary American authors such as Thomas Pynchon, Toni Morrison, Philip Roth, and Truman Capote. At the novel's inception, he addresses the reader directly, as the main character Lester Ballard is enigmatically described as a "child of God much like yourself perhaps" (4). McCarthy invites an immediate albeit tentative identification with his character: a reduced, grotesque, and monstrous aberration of humanity, who in the course of the novel violates the most sacrosanct of moral boundaries, and who with

a slow and inevitable movement will descend into a horrifying psychological oblivion. As is the case with Culla Holme, the interiors of Lester's mind are left in shadow, and readers are invited to ponder his basic identity and the circumstances that precipitate his decline. He is an outsider exiled as a child from family and community. In the context of a changing world, he has lost his home and survives by stealth, deception, and what he can glean from his skill with the rifle. But his cruelties are foreshadowed in his bullying behavior as a young boy, and malevolence seems a feature of his essential character. Surrounding him is the richly rendered natural landscape of rural Tennessee, and the nature described is simultaneously picturesque and sublime, beautiful and unremittingly harsh or indifferent. It is amid this "chaos" that Lester Ballard must survive and find purpose, and in all his depravity and brutish perversion, he seeks a connection with the human community. Again McCarthy continues his risky experiment in characterization, one that, for all his noted similarity to Faulkner, departs from his literary precursor, since in many of McCarthy's novels the minds of characters remain largely shrouded, as their motives are revealed primarily in their words and actions. The horror of Lester Ballard becomes the universal horror of human potential that an anonymous reviewer for the *Atlantic Monthly* referred to as "not inhuman, merely the far end of the continuum on which we live."[20]

The basic situation of *Child of God* is rumored to be based on an actual murder case in Sevier County, Tennessee, though there is no firm evidence to substantiate this, and the main character is reminiscent of a number of popular films of the period, including Alfred Hitchcock's *Psycho*.[21] Lester Ballard is twenty-seven years old. As a child, his mother deserted him, and his father died by suicide. The novel opens as he attempts to disrupt

an auction in which the family farm will be sold. At the auction Lester is brutally beaten with the blunt side of an axe and is taken away. He finds himself living in an abandoned cabin near his old home, and he spends his time roaming the countryside, which in McCarthy's treatment is a surreal blending of natural beauty and human waste, with its dense wooded canyons, abandoned rock quarries, and randomly disordered trash dumps. Lester travels in and out of the surrounding community, appearing briefly in stores and churches, meeting a variety of people who treat him with varying degrees of wariness and contempt. As time passes, he becomes an alien and a loner, an onlooker and a voyeur. Eventually, he finds a young man and woman dead and naked in a car. He has intercourse with the woman and takes money from the man's pocketbook. This decision sets in motion a series of murders in which the necrophiliac Lester descends further into a physical and emotional isolation, increasingly maddened by all that surrounds him, as he is uncontrollably drawn to more brutal and bizarre acts of violence and perversity.

The novel was widely reviewed and, like *Outer Dark,* evoked a passionate and rather mixed response. The disturbing and controversial subject matter received scant comment and little objection. The same anonymous reviewer in the *Atlantic Monthly* goes so far as to casually defend the novel's content, writing that "the word necrophilia has real referents in the world; no reason why it couldn't be a subject for fiction."[22] Those who reviewed the novel less enthusiastically more often objected to what they saw as ill-conceived characterization. In *Newsweek* Peter S. Prescott writes that "Cormac McCarthy's skill as a writer is not supported by his grasp of his narrative as a whole," describing Lester as "an entirely numb man." Prescott is ambivalent about the prose itself, which he sees as highly crafted and refined,

"admirably distilled," but from which "all emotion has been pared away."[23] Prescott's assessment recognizes features of the novel's tone and style that distinguish it from McCarthy's previous two novels. Though it contains little action in a conventional sense, *Child of God* is quickly paced and minimalist, with fewer archaisms and a less ornate syntax. Chapters are comparatively brief, and Lester's degeneration is precipitous and from the onset seemingly inevitable. The more critical reviews often called attention to this apparent lack of emotional force. In the *New York Times Book Review,* Richard Brickner, referring to moments in the novel when Lester's actions are described, argues that "such moments, authentic though they feel, do not much help a novel so lacking in human momentum or point." He further claims that *Child of God* is "an essentially sentimental novel that no matter how sternly it strives to be tragic is never more than morose."[24]

While many critics were concerned with what they saw as limitations in the novel's style and characterization, some considered these features the result of conscious artistic choice. In the *New Yorker,* Robert Coles, who enthusiastically reviewed *Outer Dark,* ponders McCarthy's future as an author: "one begins to wonder whether he must reach many Americans through the long, circuitous route Faulkner took: a limited recognition here, increasing response from Europeans to his strange and brooding novels, and only later the broader acknowledgment of his own countrymen."[25] Given that nearly twenty years would pass until McCarthy would achieve a wide readership and the National Book Award for *All the Pretty Horses,* there is something telling and prophetic in Coles's speculation. In the same review, he explores why the author chooses to leave Lester Ballard shrouded in mystery, less than fully comprehensible, and perhaps

somewhat thinly drawn. Coles argues: "He simply writes novels that tell us we cannot comprehend the riddles of human idiosyncrasy, the influence of the merely contingent or incidental upon our lives. He is a novelist of religious feeling who appears to subscribe to no creed but who cannot stop wondering in the most passionate and honest way what gives life meaning."[26] This recognition of McCarthy's "religious feeling," most clearly indicated by his choice of titles in his second and third novels (as well as later in *Cities of the Plain*), certainly illuminates the author's motivation for evoking the unknowable in Lester Ballard's character and for leaving the causes that circumscribe his nature in a dimly lit and barely discernible past. In the *New Republic,* in contrast to Brickner, Doris Grumbach argues that in *Child of God* McCarthy successfully inspires a deep sense of the tragic, claiming, "Again like a child of Faulkner, McCarthy is capable of black, reasonable comedy at the heart of his tragedy."[27] She further asserts that this tragic sense is universal in scope. The author "has allowed us direct communion with his special kind of chaos" since the novel offers a glimpse of "the great dark of madness and violence and inevitable death that surrounds us all."[28] Still, for all her enthusiasm, the shadow of Faulkner remains, and there are few reviewers who do not mention the name. In the *Times Literary Supplement,* in a review of *Child of God,* Roy Foster's praise for McCarthy is noteworthy. He writes that "the American South has found a powerful new voice" in which "the peculiar quality of life in the southern hills [is] distilled as rarely before" with "a sense of the tragic [that is] almost unerring." But he qualifies this praise, adding that "there is also something lacking, which Faulkner supplied: the universal vision."[29]

Though the perception of McCarthy's value at this point in his career remained compromised by his continued subjugation

to Faulkner, the setting, style, and subject matter invite the comparison. *Child of God* is certainly written in the tradition of the southern gothic, with Lester Ballard emerging as an extreme contemporary rendering of the gothic villain, a presentation of character shorn free of any lingering sense of artistic decorum that may have preceded McCarthy in the southern tradition. Ballard's perversity and the elements of the southern grotesque that attend his behavior and surroundings are common motifs and aesthetic devices in southern literature, and they continue to recall the romance tradition of the nineteenth century. The novel's structure is unconventional, organized around three primary sections. The first begins with Lester's attempt to disrupt the auction and to retain his land, and it continues as he tentatively adapts to his circumstances as an itinerant wanderer in a rural community. This first section shifts from chapters narrated in the third person (dealing with Lester's activity) to anonymous first-person chapters that reflect on Lester's character after the murders. These first-person accounts are expressed in dialect and vaguely reflect aspects of the tall tale and the tradition of Southwestern Humor, which began in the South with Augustus Baldwin Longstreet's *Georgia Scenes* (1835). The second section involves a series of chapters in third person that chart Lester's descent into depravity, beginning when he finds the asphyxiated bodies of the young couple on Frog Mountain. The third section, also in the third person, shifts between Sheriff Fate Turner's investigation and the final decline and discovery of Lester's actions.

Throughout these interlaced narrative strands, McCarthy's central concern is with Ballard himself: the source of his malevolence, its reach and potential, and the possibility of finding meaning and purpose in a world in which Lester is permitted,

even for a time, to hold violent sway. McCarthy complicates these questions by blending Lester's depravity with an unmistakable sympathy for his alienation and loss of the land, colored by the brutality and ignorance of all those he encounters. A rather epigrammatic key to Lester's character, and a place where readers are encouraged to identify with him, is when he contemplates his surroundings: "Disorder in the woods, trees down, new paths needed. Given charge Ballard would have made things more orderly in the woods and in men's souls" (136). Lester Ballard is for the most part driven by impulse, by an uncontrollable, primal, and distorted sexuality. This motive takes him to Frog Mountain to indulge his voyeurism, and it leads almost coincidentally to his descent into necrophilia. He is the personification and the dark psychological embodiment of the very chaos he apparently laments. But he is also a master of method, a survivor who for a time makes his way alone, and he plans his exploits precisely if not always successfully. A seething irony emerges after his death, when the remains of his victims are discovered in the cave in precise and "ordered" arrangement, in "a chamber in which the bodies of a number of people were arranged on stone ledges in attitudes of repose" (195). The most disturbing aspect of the novel is perhaps not the necrophilia itself but the grotesque yoking of murder, general malevolence, hatred, and sexual perversity with the innate human desire to stand against the apparent chaos of seeming forms and to build out of death itself some order and community.

These ironies and paradoxes are orchestrated through a series of brief but telling character interactions, as well as through words and the blending of complementary artistic motifs. McCarthy's language lends itself beautifully to the carnivalesque, which becomes explicit as Lester decorates his cavernous

dwelling with monstrous stuffed animals won with the rifle at carnival shooting galleries. But the carnivalesque more often appears in the author's extended descriptions, involving dark and striking costume imagery in strange color patterns, as well as settings that emphasize sensual pleasure, implying and vaguely celebrating the transgression of moral boundaries. In the first chapter, Lester is surrounded by imagery of this sort, as he stands on his porch where "wasps pass through the laddered light from the barnslats in a succession of strobic moments, gold and trembling between black and black, like fireflies in the serried upper gloom" (4). This motif becomes more direct as he attends a carnival itself, where fireworks explode like a "huge and dark Medusa," and a young girl appears in flashes of artificial light "with candyapple on her lips and her eyes wide." Her compromised innocence and implied transgression become apparent, since "her pale hair smelled of soap, womanchild from beyond the years, rapt below the sulphur glow and pitchlight of some medieval fun fair" (65). These images attend Lester's descent, and they mirror the bleak torment and disorientation that absorb him. When he is imprisoned briefly upon being accused of rape, he meets a black man, and their interchange explores the purpose of ethics given the seeming uselessness of moral agency. The black man confesses to having "cut a motherfucker's head off with a pocket knife" and claims to be "a fugitive from the ways of this world." He further laments the curse of consciousness itself and perhaps the moral laws that crystallize in the waking state, saying, "I'd be a fugitive from my mind if I had me some snow" (53). At the heart of their conversation is an embattled instinct to right action that stands in tension with the impulse compelling them to senseless acts of primal lust, perversity, and mindless violence. However tenuously, Lester clings

to a vague notion of moral order, seeking at least some cause for his errors, claiming, "All the trouble I ever was in . . . was caused by whiskey or women or both" (53). But the black man has long since abandoned any sense of ethical obligation, making no excuses and seeing no purpose in a world defined by the "chaos" that Lester weakly denies. The black man responds peremptorily, "All the trouble I ever was in was caused by getting caught" (53). This brief exchange of words illuminates the conflict that appears in Lester's few rational moments, as he seeks an ordering principle by which to judge his losses and to define the boundaries that limit his most basic impulses. This aspect of Lester's character appears in an inner "voice" of "some old shed self that came yet from time to time in the name of sanity, a hand to gentle him back from the rim of his disastrous wrath" (158). He craves human connection, even intimacy, but when he encounters it momentarily in the black man, it speaks from the abyss of violence, transgression, and disorder itself.

As the novel proceeds, the "voice" that draws him to "sanity" fades to an inaudible whisper, and the horror of Lester's behavior becomes all the more disturbing after the murders, as he clothes himself in the trappings of his victims, appearing finally as a carnival figure taken to its most grotesque extreme, a "gothic doll in illfit clothes, its carmine mouth floating detached and bright in the white landscape" (140). In stark Melvillean fashion, the interiors of Lester's fevered mind are emblematically configured in his exterior self. Lying in his cave he contemplates the mystery of his origins, seeking again a sense of place as he watches "hordes of cold stars sprawled across the smokehole" and wondering "what stuff they were made of, or himself" (141). A necrophiliac become a self-conscious caricature, he seeks retribution by ambushing the man who bought his farm.

He appears wearing women's clothing and a dry scalp taken from one of his victims, and in an exchange of gunfire he loses his arm, waking up in a hospital bed. Pursued by a mob he returns to his caves, his depravity now mirrored in gothic fashion, symbolically, in the recesses of his "grotto" (the Latin word from which "grotesque" evolves etymologically), and McCarthy describes him there: "gibbering" in "a sound not quite crying" like "the mutterings of a band of sympathetic apes" (159). This simian image stands out almost photographically, with Lester revealed as a reduced and twisted portrait of diminished humanity, and the narrative concludes in a dramatic confluence of singular events. As the apelike "child of God" emerges from the ground, a compelling moment of situational irony appears as he moves from a state of bestial isolation into a brief and fleeting connection with another human being. Crouching in the weeds beside a road, he sees himself in the face of a young boy in the window of a church bus.

McCarthy is overt in his attempt to encourage the reader's sympathy. Before Lester prepares to enact retribution on the owner of the farm his family once owned, he sits alone and apprehends the beauty of his natural surroundings, seeing "the diminutive progress of all things in the valley . . . the slow green occlusion that the trees were spreading" (170). He is drawn to despair at the cold indifference of the world: "Squatting there he let his head drop between his knees and he began to cry" (170). It is more than isolation and alienation from the human sphere that inspires this lament; it is the seeming lack of meaning implied in a nature he cannot read, an order and purpose he cannot find. In an oddly anticlimactic resolution of plot, after his escape from the mob, he returns to the hospital and is confined in a mental institution where he eventually dies. The novel ends

peremptorily, as readers are compelled to hold in memory the evocative image of transcendence Lester experiences with the boy on the road. But this flash of light is balanced by shadow, as Lester's body is dissected in the medical school and dispersed among the other cadavers, his perverse desire for connection finding gratification only in a grotesque communion with the dead. He is "laid out on a slab and flayed, eviscerated, dissected," and his various parts are "hauled forth and delineated" as the students "bent over him like those haruspices of old" (194). In a bleak irony, the order Lester seeks he embodies in death. It is here that McCarthy presents a fascinating challenge to readers, who must employ a unique interpretive practice with respect to McCarthy's use of obscure and archaic vocabulary. The novel ends with Lester as a mass of material parts, seemingly absent of spirit, implying a rigid philosophical materialism, even an antitranscendental and antireligious perspective. As doctors-in-training, the students seek to understand the nature of his physical system, its functional mechanisms and processes. But metaphorically they are also "haruspices," ancient Roman soothsayers and diviners of Etruscan origin, who read the mystic secrets in the entrails of the dead. In the end, he is a configuration of flesh, flayed and systematized, and at the same time he is a sacred text, who when read aloud speaks forth whispers of an impenetrable mystery.

Suttree (1979)

McCarthy's fourth novel, the outcome of a decade of writing and revising, is in many ways a departure from his previous work. *Suttree* is monumental in scope and length as well as detailed in its treatment of the manners, speech patterns, and the personal idiosyncrasies of multiple characters. The protagonist is

educated, a young man from a prominent Knoxville family who is alienated from his kinsmen at least in part as a matter of choice. But like *The Orchard Keeper, Outer Dark,* and *Child of God,* the novel is densely lyrical in style and unflinching in its bleak portrayal of the human scene this side of paradise. McCarthy's world remains the realm of the fallen, with elements of pathos and dark comedy blended with moments of unmediated horror and stark images of the grotesque. As with his previous novels, critical reception of the novel was seldom indifferent, with striking contrasts in perspective even in single reviews. In the *New York Times Book Review,* Jerome Charyn writes that *Suttree* has a "rude, startling power" and reads like "a doomed 'Huckleberry Finn,'" further claiming, "The book comes at us like a horrifying flood."[30] Associating the novel with Twain's masterpiece makes sense given the setting and the central role of the river as symbol. But the tense ambivalence of this characterization of *Suttree* appears in other reviews as well. In the *Washington Post,* Edward Rothstein pays particular attention to McCarthy's language, arguing that he indulges "a verbal virtuosity that runs to bloated excess" with images that are sometimes "tiresomely weighty." However, he also claims that Cornelius Suttree's adventures are "weighted with significance" since "he moves in a world so violent it nearly becomes a parody of our darkest ends."[31] Rothstein's tortured fascination with the language of *Suttree* blends with his equally reluctant acknowledgment of the novel's human texture, since amid the author's "intoxication" with "miasmatic language" (and partly as a result of it), the characters evoke a compelling sympathy: "For every horror, there is a sensitive observation. For every violent dislocation, there is a subtly touching dialogue or gesture."[32] But still it is language, style, and word choice that were

a particular preoccupation among critics. In *Esquire,* referring to McCarthy's description of the windows in a Catholic church in Knoxville, Geoffrey Wolff claims that "where words lead, McCarthy follows . . . McCarthy does not wish to show those windows . . . he likes the sound of the words he has strung together."[33] Conversely, in the *Sewanee Review,* Walter Sullivan makes a claim for language in the effective rendering of character and the world, arguing that "McCarthy's prose is so sharp and lucid that only the most determined skeptic can remain unconvinced."[34] For Sullivan it is precisely this interest in words, phrases, and the lyrical quality of well-crafted sentences that softens the bleak content of McCarthy's novels and offers a compensation for the world as the author sometimes sees it. Sullivan further argues that "McCarthy's Faulknerian prose achieves a lyricism that touches the heart and a dignity which endows some of the ugliest aspects of creation with a certain beauty."[35] Again references to the Faulknerian influence remain, blended with praise for the sensitive and precise portrayal of the distinctive settings of the American South and the characters that bring those settings to life. In the *Times Literary Supplement,* Sandra Salmans writes that "*Suttree* contains a humor that is Faulknerian in its gentle wryness, and a freakish imaginative flair reminiscent of Flannery O'Connor," ending her review with a kind of sentimental whimsy, musing that "although Suttree's eventual departure . . . is necessary, it is with a sense of regret that one watches him leave town."[36] For all the continued interest in McCarthy's language and his use of the southern grotesque, as well as with the influence of Faulkner, the most general preoccupation among initial critics appears to be the varied comic quality of scenes and the psychological texture and sympathy of the novel's many characters. This is particularly noted by Anatole

Broyard in the *New York Times,* who writes that "his people are
so vivid that they seem exotic, but this is just another way of saying that we tend to forget the range of human differences,"
claiming finally even of McCarthy's treatment of corpses: "you
won't escape his dead either. They will haunt you, which is what
they are supposed to do."[37] Thus in *Suttree,* McCarthy remains
in home territory, along the base of the Appalachians and among
the people who struggle to survive and make meaning under
harsh and even horrific conditions, but his vision becomes more
expansive in terms of social texture and human interchange,
with the blending of the urban and the rural, the comic and the
tragic. In all this he remains preoccupied with the vaguely discernable realms that transcend.

For all the breadth and scope of the novel, its structure is
fairly conventional, with thirty-four unnumbered chapters broken only by periodic spaces between paragraphs. The novel
opens, however, with an extended introduction in italics, written
in epistolary form as a direct letter to the reader that at first
belies the traditional structure that will follow. This opening
deals with setting, particularly urban Knoxville of the early
1950s, during the period just after McCarthy's own upbringing.
At this time the city had undergone a significant social and physical transformation, partially under the influence of the Tennessee
Valley Authority (TVA), from a small semi-rural town to a comparatively large industrial urban center. McCarthy is unflinch-
ingly precise in his use of the realist mode in description, as he
begins: "*Dear friend now in the dusty clockless hours of the
town when the streets lie black and steaming in the wake of the
watertrucks and now the drunk and homeless have washed up
in the lee of walls in alleys or abandoned lots*" (3). He characterizes Knoxville as a city "*constructed on no known paradigm*"

with "*a mongrel architecture reading back through the works of man in a brief delineation of the aberrant disordered and mad*" (3). But this dreamlike treatment of the physical world blends a vivid realism with a surreal quality effectively rendered through a philosophically portentous biblical language: "*The buildings stamped against the night are like a rampart to a farther world forsaken, old purposes forgot*" (3). This integration of the real and unreal is enhanced as he breaks the boundaries of time, weaving the present moment of the city's degeneration with the remote past, the age before recorded history: "*Old stone walls unplumbed by weathers, lodged in their striae fossil bones, limestone scarabs rucked in the floor of this once inland sea*" (3). The effect of this interweaving of past and present, image and idea, is to elevate setting to the level of symbol and to evoke the wasteland of medieval legend and more particularly the modern and urban "Waste Land" of T. S. Eliot's poem. The epistolary address to the reader makes clear from the novel's inception the importance of place in the author's conception, as the surreal, the gothic, the grotesque, and the carnivalesque blend in a rich integration of formal motifs and allusions.[38]

As the main narrative begins in 1951, readers are introduced to Cornelius Suttree, a willful outcast who makes a scant living as an itinerant fisherman on the Tennessee River. Partly as a result of a deep conflict with his father, having to do in part with his father's attitude to his mother's relations, he has broken with his well-placed and wealthy family, and having spent time in prison, he lives among the poor and displaced of McAnally Flats and other slum regions of the city. He is a loner of sorts, but at the same time he passively embraces the gestures of friendship offered by drunks, thieves, mussel hunters, prostitutes, transvestites, bar owners, and even a reputed witch. His most extended

relationship is with a young man he encounters first in prison and later in Knoxville after they are released. The pathetic and absurd Gene Harrogate has done time for masturbating with a farmer's watermelons and is comically referred to as "the country rat," "the city rat," and most humorously as the "midnight melon mounter." Suttree continually rescues or counsels Harrogate through the effects of his misbegotten schemes: an attempt to collect a bounty for bags of potentially rabid bats, even a plan to tunnel underneath the city through viaducts and the sewage system to rob a bank, which ends in an explosion with Harrogate pathetically mired in human waste. In all this, Suttree emerges as an unlikely paternal figure, the one human being these outcasts can turn to in moments of desperation. He reluctantly transgresses moral boundaries when the immediacy of human need calls for it; yet readers learn of his own guilt after abandoning his wife and child and being sent to prison. This becomes clear as he visits his estranged wife at the child's funeral and is repulsed by her family and sent away by the local sheriff. The novel develops as a directionless journey through the external wasteland of urban Knoxville and the interior wasteland of Suttree's tortured consciousness, culminating finally in a dream vision under the effects of typhoid fever and his ultimate decision to leave the city behind. Again *Suttree* evokes elements of the southern gothic and grotesque, the American historical and metaphysical romance, and it recalls the essentially modern concerns and settings, even the formal structures of James Joyce's *Ulysses,* a novel with which it has often been compared.

Unlike McCarthy's previous works, *Suttree* draws from the conventions of the American city novel, which emerged as a fully constituted subgenre in the later half of the nineteenth century. With its emphasis on economic scarcity, competition,

social texture and density, as well as urban degradation, the novel recalls the realism of Rebecca Harding Davis's "Life in the Iron Mills" (1861) and William Dean Howells's *The Rise of Silas Lapham* (1885). More particularly and perhaps more plausibly, it derives in part from the naturalism of Stephen Crane's *Maggie: A Girl of the Streets* (1893), Theodore Dreiser's *Sister Carrie* (1900), *An American Tragedy* (1925), and *The Financier* (1912), as well as the great urban novels of Sinclair Lewis, Upton Sinclair, and the displaced southerner Thomas Wolfe. Available biographical information does not reveal specific evidence that McCarthy was steeped in these writers, but their works were highly respected and immensely popular in the eras just preceding McCarthy's emergence as a novelist, and the social texture and thematic preoccupations of *Suttree* suggest an influence. In *Suttree,* as in all these urban novels, the city emerges as a subject of immense preoccupation, as the essential reality that defines the protagonist, conditions in part his identity, and circumscribes his range of choices both ethical and otherwise. Knoxville is darkly vivid: "In the lobbies of the slattern hotels the porters and bellmen are napping in the chairs and lounges, dark faces jerking in their sleep down the worn wine plush. In the rooms lie drunken homecome soldiers sprawled in painless crucifixion on the rumpled counterpanes and the whores are sleeping now" (27). Young Suttree is a part of this world, as he participates in the drunken routs of his dubious comrades, seeks with some desperation various ways to feed and clothe himself, and near the end finds brief emotional repose in a relationship with a prostitute who initially comforts him but eventually becomes emotionally unstable. Still, McCarthy's use of the various conventions of the city novel is blended with the formal features of the American romance in a richly lyrical language that is most

often suggestive of unknowable realms beyond the social and the material.

This appears as he evokes the essential tensions of the American historical romance. Though *Suttree* was published in 1979 and is set less than thirty years earlier, the conflict between the forces of progress and reaction (a thematic strand in the historical romance from James Fenimore Cooper to William Faulkner and clearly seen in *The Orchard Keeper*) is central to the conditions young Suttree faces. In the context of the novel, the urban development projects of the Tennessee Valley Authority give rise to the modern city, transforming and at times destroying the rural landscape as well as the social institutions and traditions of the mountain communities. At the same time they initiate important and useful material developments, driving people like Gene Harrogate to the city to seek the opportunities provided there. Still, in the end these opportunities offer them only the degraded reality of McAnally Flats, the polluted river corrupted with industrial waste, floating condoms, and refuse in rich profusion, even the grotesque images of aborted fetuses and, in one instance (reminiscent of *Outer Dark*), the drifting body of a dead infant. Progress with all its dubious implications is presented in the light of a stark and garish reality.

Cornelius Suttree's wanderings involve a metaphysical quest with an intensely ethical dimension, and to orchestrate this pattern McCarthy makes use of overarching structural motifs drawn from the wasteland of Christian and medieval legend and the underworld journey of the ancient Greek, Roman, and medieval epics. These elaborate image systems enrich the stark realism of the novel and blend with the more psychologically and philosophically textured elements of the American romance tradition. Suttree's alienation from family and self-understanding becomes

simultaneously a removal from time, history, and the particular material preoccupations of the present, as he becomes, like all epic protagonists, a representative man confronting the essential human condition, characterized by existential isolation and metaphysical dread. These are timeless concerns that take on a particular gravity in the twentieth century, during the modernist period, and the images McCarthy evokes recall T. S. Eliot's post–World War I London, as seen in book 2 of "The Waste Land" (1922). Eliot writes, "A rat crept softly through the vegetation / Dragging its slimy belly on the bank / While I was fishing in the dull canal / On a winter evening round behind the gashouse."[39] It is a telling parallel that, like Suttree, the persona in this section of the poem identifies himself as a fisherman, and in *Suttree,* this same urban decay and degradation is intensified: "The viaduct spanned a jungly gut filled with rubble and wreckage and a few packingcrate shacks inhabited by transient blacks and down through this puling waste the dark and leprous waters of First Creek threaded the sumac and poison ivy. Highwater marks of oil and sewage and condoms dangling in the branches like stranded leeches" (116). This description of the city is vivid and precise, marked by an intense realism, as seen in the "wreckage," the "shacks," as well as the "oil" and "sewage." But these images are heightened and contextualized through a biblical language imbued with an unmistakable mythic resonance. This appears in the lyrical arrangement of words and in images such as the "puling waste" and the "dark and leprous waters." These combine to integrate reality and nightmare, as the waters of purification have become the carriers of disease, with the surrounding trees displaying the "condoms dangling," connoting displaced and unproductive desire and perverse and ill-gotten fulfillment. In all this the natural and generative order of nature

has been corrupted by the forces of modern industrial "progress." These images mirror the confusion and alienation of Cornelius Suttree himself. This appears as he makes direct contact with the city and the polluted environment that surrounds it, and as the scene blends with his own distorted perception and limited understanding: "Suttree pressed on, down the carious undersides of the city, through black and slaverous cavities where foul liquors seeped. He had not known how hollow the city was" (276). The world he confronts becomes more than a material realm of degradation brought to bleak fruition by human avarice. It is that, most certainly, but it is also a complex emblem of an existential void, a hollow wilderness bereft of light and possibility.

Suttree's descent into darkness is intensified further as it displays the features of the underworld journey. His status as a modern antihero of a particular and more stalwart kind appears as the underworld is portrayed in explicit terms, as "he began to suspect some dimensional displacement in these descents to the underworld, some disparity unaccountable between the above and the below," and as the Tennessee River itself—reminiscent of the River Styx in Greek mythology, Dante's *Divine Comedy,* and Milton's *Paradise Lost*—is lined in trees where "bats hung in clusters like bunches of dark and furry fruit and the incessant drip of water echoed everywhere through the spelaean dark like dull chimes" (262). Blending with this unambiguous underworld scene are features of the grotesque, as well as beautiful images of primordial nature transformed as if permanently into seemingly crystalline aesthetic objects: "In the pools lay salamanders cold and prone and motionless as terracotta figurines" (262). The effect of this use of the wasteland, the underworld, and the literary grotesque is to display in vivid terms the irreducible texture

of the world Suttree must contend with, to provide a context for a journey rife with confusion, dread, and gothic horror and at the same time replete with images of the sublime, with supernal beauty and transcendent mystery. But Suttree's is not a journey of physical isolation alone, since his wanderings take him to McAnally Flats, through the streets of the town, down the river, and, almost beyond choosing, make him an essential part of a human scene replete with comedy and bittersweet pathos. This occurs as he encounters characters such as J-Bone, Junior, Bobby-john, Bearhunter, Boneyard, Hoghead, Oceanfrog, Smokehouse, and Gatemouth, among others. Lost and degraded as these characters are, they form an unlikely family, a jovial community of the fallen, and each of them clings to Suttree ("Sut," as they often affectionately call him) as a means of grounding their desperate lives. Thus, the horror and hopeless dread of this urban underworld finds its counterpoint in the ever-present possibility of human connection and intimacy.

As the novel proceeds, this densely social realm is enriched by the interiors of Suttree's mind and the metaphysical dread and preoccupation implied in the wasteland and underworld iconography. After the departure of his prostitute lover, he is stricken with typhoid fever, and the novel reaches its penultimate phase in a lengthy dream both nightmarish and comic, carnivalesque in its imagery and starkly grotesque. He is found in a state of delirium by his friend J-Bone, and his carnival vision takes shape as he sees "Father Bones," who "tilts out through saloon doors and is gone, old varnished funhouse skeleton" (450). With a touching concern for his highly contagious friend, J-Bone takes him to the hospital where his fevered dream is heightened by an injection of morphine, becoming a surreal and sometimes nightmarish encounter with a realm beyond the material world, "a cold

dimension without time without space and where all is motion"
(452). He moves from the world of tactile reality into a middle
realm in which the real is altered and distorted, suggestive of
forces beyond normal waking comprehension, where "an enor-
mous white doctor crossed his vision and drew away" (453). As
others come in and out of his room, he sees them as "bald
bipedal mutants struggling down there on the raw and livid rim
of consciousness with a sad amusement" (453) Whether it is a
product of Suttree's tortured consciousness or not, the dream
vision takes on religious overtones that will culminate in his
encounter with a priest after he awakens, and in the midst of his
delusion his thoughts are precise and evocative, as "his astro-
nomical bias placed him beyond the red shift and he wondered
at the geography of these spaces or how does the world mesh
with the world beyond the world?" (453). His vision deepens
into a pure dream, void of present reality, and his tortured guilt,
partly motivated by a latent sense of obligation to his family,
leads to a brief comic trial and an oddly distanced encounter
with his friends in McAnally Flats, which seems only to precede
his descent through the "gates of Hades." This portentous nightmare ends only as he weakly awakens, stands, and is soon found
by a nurse who helps him back to bed. She encourages him to
stay silent, but dramatically and succinctly he reveals to her the
elliptical content of his strange epiphany: "I have a thing to tell
you. I know all souls are one and all souls lonely" (459). The
experience is transformative if paradoxical, and his sobered perspective at its conclusion suggests the intensity of its effect upon
him. He must live and cope with his own isolation, even as he
courts the reality of metaphysical realms beyond the sensory.
This becomes clear with the priest who offers to hear his confession. The priest gives him a drop of wine and says that God

himself must have been watching over him, and Suttree responds, "You would not believe what watches" (461). Respectful of his experience as if he knows it was more than a dream, the priest asks if that is what he has learned, and Suttree responds, "I learned that there is one Suttree and one Suttree only" (461), and he follows this statement with a chilling claim: "The days were long and lonely, no one came" (462). This is a painfully ambiguous experience rife with dread, and the truth of the dream itself, which is the result of physical sickness and tortured guilt, must be weighed against other metaphysical and religious experiences that suggest many possibilities. This appears specifically in his encounter with the ragman, as well as in a brief moment of illumination that follows the dream vision, and in the startling imagery of the novel's conclusion.

The ragman is typical of many of McCarthy's peasant mystics, an old man tempered by the reality of his experiences, endowed with an oblique wisdom and repose that allows him to ponder the mysteries of the universe with a fearless blend of skepticism and reverence. He lives along the river in a cavern beneath a bridge, where he observes the varied scenes and the people who pass by. Suttree encounters him with some regularity and is drawn to him as a kindred spirit and fellow traveler. In one scene, the ragman speaks warily of the many tragic events that have come before his eyes: a lynching in Georgia from the back of a springwagon; a cyclone that drained the river dry, destroying homes and scattering possessions. From all this, he calmly accepts his own impending death, and together they ponder its ultimate meaning. Suttree asks him what, if anything, happens beyond the grave, and the ragman responds, "Don't nothin happen. You're dead" (258). But Suttree reminds him that he once believed in God. The ragman remembers and

answers only with "maybe," musing on the idea that if he ever sees God face to face, he will ask why he was subjected to the "crapgame" of human experience. The ragman ends his imaginary conversation concluding that even God must struggle with the irreducible mysteries of his own creation. Referring to his question about the meaning of the crapgame, the ragman says: "I don't believe he can answer it. . . . I don't believe there is an answer" (258). The philosophical weight of this statement is easy to miss but essential to the religious texture of the novel, and it is here we find McCarthy, for all his interest in science, pondering the limitations of what he seemingly views as a naïveté inherent in scientific positivism taken to the extreme. He also calls attention to the rigidly circumscribed limitations embedded in religious traditions. No quest for ultimate knowledge yields the complete answer because in a fundamental way this answer is unavailable. Materialist and positivist readings of the ragman's words are inadequate, since they claim to firmly respond to the question of human suffering with the indifference of natural law, perhaps in the context of purely materialist applications of Darwinian evolution. Through these false interpretations the question finds affirmation in a purified scientific materialism. But answers drawn from the varied religious traditions, especially those that implicitly reduce the mysteries of the cosmos, presume also to find solace in a different form of certitude, but a certitude nevertheless. McCarthy's skepticism is radical, deeper and more expansive, reminiscent of Herman Melville's skepticism, transcending intellectual, philosophical, and religious systems.

But here readers may begin to observe a thematic strand that the author will carry through his many later novels and dramatic works, occasionally in *Blood Meridian* and the Border Trilogy,

and most notably in *The Road* and *The Sunset Limited*. Ever the eclectic philosophical writer, McCarthy entertains something similar to a "panentheist" worldview, which contrasts markedly with traditional Judeo-Christian "theism" and the more contemporary "pantheism" of many varied modern perspectives widely held. It is quite similar to the Existential Christianity rooted in Søren Kierkegaard, Paul Tillich, Rudolph Bultmann, John Macquarrie, and even Fyodor Dostoyevsky. "Theism" posits a divine realm that exists outside the natural realm and briefly intercedes in the world, in events seen as "super"-natural. "Pantheism" involves the notion of a godhead fully embedded in the natural world, in the end reducing "divinity" to the impersonal and material. "Panentheism" (defined in the *OED* as "The theory or belief that God encompasses and interpenetrates the universe but at the same time is greater and independent of it") is a term first employed by the German philosopher Karl Christian Friedrich Krauss (1781–1832) and is commonly associated in the twentieth century with the theologian Charles Hartshorne (1897–2000). It derives from the Greek *pan* meaning "everything," *en* meaning "in," and *theos* meaning "God." Though the term is comparatively new, the essential ideas of panentheism are expressed in a range of contexts both ancient and modern: in early native North and South American cultures as well as in the fifth-century B.C.E. works of Heraclitus (ca. 535–475 B.C.E.). These ideas influenced the development of early Christian theology, especially in the Eastern Orthodox Church, and continue in the West as an important strand of theological reflection. This line of thinking runs alongside a popular myth-based traditional theism, one that points to a storied "God of miracles" who exists outside of His creation, interceding in occasional moments of miraculous intervention. In this Christian context, panentheism

is attributed to Saint Paul in Acts 17:28, where God is seen as the one in whom "we live and move and have our being." This worldview posits the notion of the universe as a physical reality contained within the body of God, who is a fully constituted being present within the physical but in equal measure transcending it. Practically, this benevolent divinity may be glimpsed in moments of human intimacy and concerns that reveal themselves even under the darkest of circumstances. After Suttree's dream vision, as he leaves town, he encounters the comic and endearing transvestite Tripping Through The Dew. After she/he offers to help with money, Suttree leaves pondering his own identity and purpose. Finding his Catholicism inadequate to explain his encounters with the world as well as his glimpses of the metaphysical, he discards "the little cloaked godlet and his other amulets in a place where they would not be found in his lifetime," taking "for talisman the simple human heart within him" (468). Any rejection of the divine implied in Suttree's penultimate reflection is firmly mitigated by the explicit metaphysical quality that defines the novel's conclusion. It is through the redemptive possibilities of the "simple human heart" that the divine becomes incarnate, a theme more fully explored in later works, especially in the words of Black, the urban street preacher in *The Sunset Limited*. McCarthy darkens and alters this pantheist perspective into something distinctly his own, by concluding *Suttree* with the fearful image of the mysterious huntsman. Beneficent panentheism is radically altered as the author foregrounds the reality of an evil that transcends and must be understood along with the good. But pure materialism disappears in an unambiguous emanation from beyond the physical world: "Somewhere in the gray wood by the river is the

huntsman and in the brooming corn and in the castellated press of cities. His work lies all wheres and his hounds tire not. I have seen them in a dream, slaverous and wild and their eyes crazed with ravening for souls in this world. Fly them" (471).

The many encounters and moments of intimacy in the novel are a testimony to the redemptive power of Suttree's heart, and his actions transform lives and provide a form of healing. Before the huntsman is seen, McCarthy heightens the blending of material and spiritual elements. Like Lester Ballard, Suttree experiences a binding connection with a human being, as a boy offers him a drink of water from a pail, and Suttree encounters his own image in the "smoking cobalt" of the child's eyes, which are "blue . . . with no bottoms like the sea" (471). Counterbalancing the darkness of his dream vision, this experience involves a paradoxical encounter with both the transcendent and the immanent, with sublime beauty and humanity, but it must be accepted alongside the supernal darkness of the huntsman's tireless hounds, who transcend time and seek ravenously for the souls of all who live. Thus the novel, with biblical language and mythic resonance, seeks to contain elaborate systems of contraries while exploring if not reconciling the essential contradictions of a world defined by love and violence, predation and healing, body and spirit, and isolation and human connection.

Into the West
Blood Meridian

In the late 1970s Cormac McCarthy moved from Knoxville to El Paso and began research on a new novel rooted in the troubling history of westward expansion. This work would unmask the romantic assumptions that informed the mythology of the western genre and the politics of Manifest Destiny, bringing an obscure and violent moment to life and lifting the events out of the nineteenth century, casting them into the realm of the universal. In this sweeping context, questions of good and evil, morality and malevolence, and the very issue of human purpose are brought into sharp relief, all against the stark and exquisite beauty of a new setting—the American West. *Blood Meridian; or, The Evening Redness in the West* (1985) is an arresting novel that blends all the author's influences, recalling Shakespeare, Melville, Faulkner, and Dostoyevsky, echoing the tone of the King James Bible and Dante's *Divine Comedy*. Infusing this strange alchemy of tradition are McCarthy's distinctive lyrical style and his intense concern with the extremes of human experience. The governing motive of much of the author's work, especially *Blood Meridian,* is the question of meaning, purpose, and value in a universe that yields answers only in bright but fleeting glimpses. Can human beings speak of possibility, hope, even God, with any validity or intellectual credibility? Can the assumptions of inherent meaning reflected in the dominant

world religions be entertained with any honesty by the twentieth-century mind? Though the novel recounts events in the 1850s, it is born of modern memory—from a sensibility conditioned by two world wars, the physical and psychological effects of genocide, the devastation of colonialism and environmental waste, as well as the collective anxiety of the nuclear age. In *Blood Meridian*, questions of meaning and the nature and possibility of the divine are addressed, not under conditions of benevolence and repose, but under the observable extremes of human violence and the brutal deterministic forces of the natural world. If true hope exists, it must be found amid these conditions, and if revealed, it is a stalwart and lasting hope indeed. McCarthy does not presume to provide coherent answers through an alternative worldview. He does not firmly reject traditional Judeo-Christian and Classical assumptions and replace them with a fashionable nihilism articulated through absurdist renderings of the human scene. His approach reflects a deeper gravity and ambiguity, and among many of his contemporaries he is unique in his manner of presentation and thematic texture. In *Blood Meridian,* he adopts and modifies the narrative strategies of Melville and Dostoyevsky by giving voice to multiple perspectives. The possibility of a universe absent of transcendent meaning is considered, together with the present potential of a creation dominated by evil. But alive as well in the world of *Blood Meridian* is the ubiquitous "voice" that binds the physical and spiritual into mysterious unity and reveals itself through discrete gestures of human decency and benevolence. It is this richness of perspective that led Harold Bloom to place *Blood Meridian* among the greatest works of twentieth-century literature. In 2006 a survey conducted by the *New York Times* echoed these sentiments, judging

the novel as one of the five finest written by a contemporary American author.

Understanding this work, however, requires that readers come to terms with the varied traditions in the novel form that McCarthy employs, and one must understand that the language presented in various monologues is overtly philosophical, intentionally vague and evasive, inviting multiple readings and considerations. In terms of structure, *Blood Meridian* shares with *Outer Dark* a trim and coherent narrative line, with twenty-eight chapters and an epilogue, each chapter preceded by bolded highlights of major events. The form is episodic, and typical of the picaresque tradition, it centers on the exploits of an outsider figure who observes as much as participates in the tortured moral complexities that define the human situation. Its central protagonist is the unnamed "kid," a fourteen-year-old runaway who in 1849 abandons his alcoholic father (a bereft schoolmaster) and in striking similarity to Huckleberry Finn "lights out for the Territory." In spite of his father's education, the kid can neither read nor write (a sign of neglect), and as he travels west he soon nourishes "a taste for mindless violence" (3). After a brief tour with a marauding army troop in which he survives an attack by Comanches, he finds himself traveling with the infamous Glanton Gang. Here McCarthy draws on actual history, specifically from a narrative account of the gang's horrific exploits written by a participant, Samuel Chamberlain, entitled *My Confessions: The Recollections of a Rogue*. In this memoir, Chamberlain provides portraits of many of the central characters of the novel, including John Joel Glanton and more important the Texas outlaw Judge Holden. *Blood Meridian* takes Chamberlain's essential prototypes and from the scant data provided creates fully rendered literary characters, elevating them to

mythic and densely philosophical proportions. Tellingly the kid's initial experience of the events that will define him occurs in the east Texas town of Nacogdoches, which is located on the ninety-eighth meridian, identified by Frederick Jackson Turner as the boundary line that separates the frontier and the wilderness. This is where he meets the judge, who is seven feet tall, bald and cold white, an extraordinary man of monstrous physical and intellectual stature. The judge is an expert rhetorician, and in a bold stroke he erroneously exposes an itinerant preacher as a fraud and a reprobate. Soon he reveals himself as a master of languages, philosophy, religion, natural history, and geography. He is a figure as erudite as he is perverse, becoming the bleak counterpoint to the conventional western hero. In literary terms the judge recalls Melville's white whale and Captain Ahab, as well as Dostoyevsky's Grand Inquisitor, Milton's Satan, Shakespeare's Iago, and the extraliterary character of the Marquis de Sade. From a religious and philosophical perspective, the judge's many pronouncements throughout the novel reflect the Nietzschean *Übermensch* (Superman), Satan of the Old and New Testaments, Job's comforters, the evil archons or the demiurge of ancient Gnosticism, and he is perhaps most obviously the dark avatar of scientific positivism—in this case of the Enlightenment gone horribly astray.[1] In artfully blending these various conceptions and figurations, he becomes a uniquely contemporary villain, one who espouses a brutish philosophy that McCarthy presents as the ethical outcome of a rigid philosophical materialism. Sometime after his initial encounter with the judge, the kid finds himself traveling with Glanton, the judge, and his outlaw band of scalp hunters who collect a government bounty for Apaches but who indiscriminately murder peaceful Indians and Mexicans. In the process, the kid unwillingly becomes the

judge's protégé, and between them stands the former priest Tobin, a man who both admires and loathes Judge Holden and all he represents. Each character becomes an interlocutor in a deadly verbal battle, one in which ethics and their absence frame the interchange, and even death stands pale against the potential decimation of human souls.

Among many scholars *Blood Meridian* has emerged as McCarthy's masterpiece, but initial reviews were relatively scant and perplexing. Perhaps the author's change of locale—from the South to the West—led to a certain confusion and uninterest. It may be that the six years between *Suttree* and *Blood Meridian* obscured McCarthy from critical view. Ironically it was in these intervening years that he received the "Genius Grant," "the prestigious MacArthur Fellowship, and was considered by many in the literary establishment (even before his move to the West) as one of the most important authors of his generation. But reviewers in many of the major magazines and newspapers simply missed or ignored the novel. Those who considered it were generally ambivalent and understandably disoriented by the extreme rendering of violence as well as the perplexing blend of horrific description and philosophical pronouncement. In the *Sewanee Review,* Walter Sullivan poses the question quite pointedly: "What do we make of this phenomenon, a mind that dwells unremittingly on evil and a prose that conveys these thoughts with the tongue of an angel?"[2] Sullivan strikes at the heart of an essential paradox inherent in any response to McCarthy's work in general—one must reconcile the lyrical power of the author's language and narrative style, which blends words and imagery in a remarkable alchemy of the sublime and the picturesque, with a rendering of violence and depravity largely unparalleled in Western literature. This integration of

aesthetic beauty and horror is unsettling to say the least, and *Blood Meridian* must remain for some unapproachable. For others, it is an experience to be encountered once, while some consider and reconsider the novel for its fascinating but ultimately inaccessible depths. Still, Walter Sullivan, whose initial response was contrary to that of scholars who later worked in detail with the text, saw it as limited in scope, since its "savage code circles back to the theme of survival, which does not seem to me to be theme enough."[3] He further challenges the novel's structure, claiming that it is "very weak."[4] In the *New York Times Book Review,* Caryn James expresses similar concerns, arguing that *Blood Meridian* reveals "a passionate voice given equally to ugliness and lyricism." She admits that there are no answers to the issues McCarthy confronts but suggests that "there are more rigorous, coherent ways to frame the questions." Finally, she concludes that "if 'Blood Meridian' is ultimately a failure, it is an ambitious, sophisticated one."[5] Critics acknowledged that the task of integrating American history, art, and philosophy is formidable for any author, and reviews, even when negative, were forgiving and respectful, especially of McCarthy's multiple ambitions. In the *Times Literary Supplement,* Andrew Hislop strikes a measured pose, noting that the novel is written in a "rich style, both colloquial and bookish, with biblical echoes of times when the word and blood were rhetorically joined." He encourages readers to see beneath the surface reality of human depravity, arguing that the work is "much more than a counterblast of bloody imagery against more cosy perceptions of the West. It is an exploration, at times explicitly philosophical, of the relationship between culture and violence."[6] In the *Appalachian Journal,* perhaps because he is both a reviewer and a McCarthy scholar, Edwin T. Arnold anticipates critical trends that continue to the

present day. He claims that McCarthy is fascinated by "sin in its most shocking and virulent forms" and is "innately distrustful of sweetness and sentimentality," further arguing that *Blood Meridian* must be considered in historical context as "an indictment of the whole Western philosophy of Manifest Destiny, of moral and cultural rightness which has ruled our country from the Pilgrims to Vietnam, Nicaragua, and beyond."[7] For all the perplexity and ambivalence in these early reviews, each recognized the novel's formal and thematic density, the richness of language, and the sweeping range of its historical, philosophical, and religious concerns.

Genre

Blood Meridian is in many ways similar to T. S. Eliot's "The Waste Land" (1922). It is simultaneously traditional and experimental, innovative yet evocative of many classic works in the Western tradition. As in *The Orchard Keeper* and *Outer Dark*, McCarthy draws from the conventions of the American historical romance and the metaphysical romances of Herman Melville. Like Melville and Dostoyevsky, he employs a narrative technique largely specific to the novel form, one that permits an interplay of perspectives, attitudes, and disparate and sometimes contradictory themes, through multiple character monologues and the intervention of a third-person narrative voice that interweaves objective and subjective modes of perception. In his use of the American historical romance, *Blood Meridian* explicitly engages the popular national frontier mythology that begins with the novels of James Fenimore Cooper and finds its modern expression in western novels and films. Complicating this popular genre, however, characters such as the kid and the judge retain the iconic and larger-than-life status of myth, but

McCarthy's treatment of their nature is openly revisionist, questioning and even flagrantly dismantling the values that define the frontier hero. In an important series of studies dealing with this figure in narrative, novel, and film, Richard Slotkin charts the complexities of American mythology from the eighteenth century to the present. In *Gunfighter Nation: The Myth of the Frontier in Twentieth-Century America,* Slotkin identifies a significant reconfiguration of the western genre in film, roughly coinciding with the birth of the nuclear age, taking on an increased urgency in the cold war and the post-Vietnam eras. He calls the various works of this new genre "alternative westerns" in the revisionist mode.[8] *Blood Meridian* emerges in this time frame, in the wake of the films of Sergio Leone, Sam Peckinpah, and the especially popular dark revisionist features of Clint Eastwood, and McCarthy enriches this alterative tradition through the novel form. Central to these modern treatments of western history is a direct and honest portrayal of human avarice and depravity.

In the context of this revisionist approach, readers' discomfort with and objections to McCarthy's treatment of violence, which may be articulated from a moral and an aesthetic point of view, must be considered in the context of the historical events McCarthy brings to light. Chamberlain's memoir is thinly rendered, but the historical reality of the events is largely verifiable, both in terms of the specific individuals portrayed and other historical incidents of a similar nature. Given McCarthy's debt to the American romance tradition, particularly its nineteenth-century manifestation, it is illuminating to consider the issue of violence in *Blood Meridian* in the context of Nathaniel Hawthorne's "Roger Malvin's Burial" (1832). In this tale set in 1725, Hawthorne tells the tragic story of two combatants in the French and

Indian War who participated in the celebrated "Lovell's Fight," in which Captain John Lovewell (in an act of revenge) led an attack on the Pequawket Indians of southwestern Maine. Though "Lovell's Fight" ended in defeat, in striking parallel to the events in *Blood Meridian,* Lovewell's men were previously offered a bounty for scalps, and they indiscriminately slaughtered other human beings for material gain. In subsequent years, their exploits were widely celebrated in patriotic terms. While none of these events appears in Hawthorne's story, and the main characters express themselves in the language of chivalry and self-sacrifice, the horror of their unnamed actions resonates in the form of the nineteenth-century romance as an important subtext, and it is perhaps reflected in the tortured guilt that destroys the life of the main character, Reuben Bourne. In *Blood Meridian,* a late-twentieth-century novel written in a time when the conventions of artistic decorum have undergone a radical shift, McCarthy simply lifts the veil, revealing the darker realities of American conquest in explicit terms.

The precise location of the novel's initial setting, on the ninety-eighth meridian, which marks the western edge of Euro-American civilization, firmly establishes the narrative as a frontier romance and invites the consideration of many of the formal, aesthetic, and thematic implications central to the genre. As in *The Orchard Keeper,* the forces of progress and reaction are in dynamic play, as the dark principles and malevolent agents of civilization decimate the land. At least initially, Glanton and Judge Holden are on solid working terms with the government of Texas, and the judge is presented as having sat with the governor recalling memories of the great European cities, speaking playfully and fluently in French. The gang works directly in the interest of the civil body politic, clearing away the violent and

uncivilized natives that stand in the way of progress and civilization. In his eloquence, learning, aesthetic sense and appreciation, as well as his rhetorical charisma, the judge ironically displays the best ideals of refinement associated with Western culture from the Classical Age to the Enlightenment. The fact that he appears also as an unspeakable villain suggests that the novel's historical revisionism is single-minded in its critical attitude toward westward expansionism, as both the violent and the peaceful among the native populations are obliterated by Glanton's and Judge Holden's indiscriminate bloodlust and greed. This reading is valid, but it must be taken alongside a deeper skepticism in the novel's texture that transcends history, culture, and politics, since McCarthy's treatment of the world resonates with a deeper quasi-religious, even biblical language. This language invites the supposition that the evil manifest in the gang and their leaders is not exclusive to them or to the political and economic interests they represent. Walter Sullivan's recognition of the "evil" and the "angelic" in McCarthy's works is revealed most fully early in the novel as the kid witnesses an attack of Comanches who descend upon the army troop as if from another world. The author's extended description is modern and explicitly surreal. The nightmarish quality of the passage lifts the event out of local history, and the bloody conflict echoes the apocalyptic imagery of the book of Revelation.

The attack appears as more than a single incident, evoking former battles in other places and times, and the event as a whole becomes a sweeping metaphorical rendering of the violence that has defined not only human history but the history of the physical universe itself. The natives are garbed in "the coats of slain dragoons" and "the pieces of uniform still tracked with the blood of prior owners" (52). Older conflicts appear in the stolen

clothing worn by the Comanches, in "the breastplate and pauldrons deeply dented with old blows of mace and saber done in another country by men whose very bones were dust" (52). The surreal quality in these descriptions of dress not only places the narrative in a region out of time, through a dreamlike imagery and a fluid and lyrical prose, it reimagines linear time by blending highly specific but disparate historical references, thus making the horrid violence that defines the moment a reality present throughout the course of human history. The claim here is not rigidly philosophical or scientific but obliquely religious, since the costumes themselves are "attic or biblical" (52), recalling both the Greco-Roman Classical and the Judaic past, and the natives emerge into view as "a legion of horribles . . . riding down upon them like a horde from a hell more horrible yet than the brimstone land of christian reckoning" (53). This apocalyptic scene concludes in an unparalleled crescendo of madness and violence, a stark example of the literary grotesque that appears through an intricate blend of opposites—lyrical language, historical references, color, detail, a rich integration of biblical allusion, together with horrific violence and nightmare reality. At a universal level, the event as presented suggests a brutish passion and malevolence that transcends cultures and civilizations, oceans and continents, as well as time and human history. While the subsequent actions of the gang must rightfully be read as an indictment of American expansionism and Manifest Destiny, the attack of Comanches, perhaps the most extended and powerful description McCarthy had written to date, appears early in the novel at the conclusion of chapter 4. All the actions that follow in *Blood Meridian* must be read with this event in mind. Thus McCarthy's revisionism takes aim not just at late-nineteenth-century American progressivism, but at the natives themselves,

who manifest the same depravity as their eventual conquerors. The primary target of the author's hard visionary indictment is human nature, as well as any ideology—scientific, social, or religious—that would claim that human perfectibility is in any way remotely attainable. In the political terms of the American historical romance, the implications are not entirely clear. The civilizing motives of American culture are dubious and oddly regressive, even brutal and avaricious. But since the novel is read in retrospect, in the context of a comparatively stable twentieth-century American security, the rule of law that would prohibit these impulses from full expression seems an absolute necessity, and civilizations by their very nature construct moral foundations from statutory frameworks of this sort. In this sense, McCarthy's revisionist "alternative western" is distinctive, nuanced, and ambiguous in the political values that inform events and characters.

Another feature of the American historical romance is the evocative description of American landscape, and *Blood Meridian* is replete with extended treatments of nature that are detailed and poetic, as McCarthy explores the connection between the natural laws that govern the land and the thinking creatures that live interdependently in relation to it. Ever the writer conscious of his antecedents in the American literary tradition, he draws heavily from his predecessors among the American naturalists, particularly Jack London and later Ernest Hemingway. This naturalism is specifically expressed in the notion of "optical democracy," a concept that appears as McCarthy writes of a bleak Texas scene: "in the optical democracy of such landscapes all preference is made whimsical and a man and a rock become endowed with unguessed kinships" (247). This concept involves a leveling of the traditional hierarchy that

would assert the primacy of human beings, their separation from the natural world, even their capacity to transcend. McCarthy's notion of "optical democracy" provides a gloss on a series of wonderfully detailed passages that some critics have cited as indicative of a rigid and stark determinism, one that asserts the primacy of the material world, the dominance of natural law, the fundamental indifference of nature, and the absence of any transcendent presence or meaning. The novel foregrounds, with a gravity and force many find difficult to absorb, the suffering that ensues as life confronts life, and the material confronts the material, in a phenomenal realm in which no single species or no individual organism holds primary sway. On the surface, if any single dominance is to be found, it is in Judge Holden himself, who maintains his force and control because he alone recognizes the laws that bind, the laws of will and violence that at least metaphorically make a deity of malevolent destruction. The thematic tie that links the judge to antireligious materialism and philosophical naturalism becomes clear in his many monologues, in which he reveals himself as a natural historian and an avatar of Enlightenment science. As the Marquis de Sade (in his embrace of personal freedom in sexual perversion) can be seen as the political outcome of individualistic positivism taken to the darkest extreme, so the judge can be seen as a potential result of the assertions of a modern science taken to the philosophical extreme, which privilege the phenomenal over the numinous, the material over the transcendent. But it is in the very mystery that attends his character that an ambiguous Romantic sensibility must inform our reading of the novel in general. His very indomitability suggests that he represents, connotes, even manifests a mysterious force beyond the physical world, a force that works as the primary energy that drives the engine of material

nature. The optical democracy that appears in the novel in various descriptions of nature is integrated with the richly rendered character of Judge Holden to create a balance between naturalist materialism in its most extreme intellectual form and the dark romantic tradition that engages the question of cosmological mystery, metaphysics, and the sublime. Thus, the American historical romance, with its use of the mythic hero and descriptions of nature on the frontier, is employed to a rich variety of thematic ends.

Philosophical Themes and Ethical Concerns

In McCarthy's hands the American historical romance becomes more openly philosophical in nature, and the novel emerges in part from the influence of McCarthy's favorite works, Herman Melville's *Moby-Dick* and Fyodor Dostoyevsky's *The Brothers Karamazov*. All three novels share a preoccupation with unanswerable questions related to the existence, nature, and role of the divine, as well as with the possibility of transcendence through human action and benevolence. The force of the judge as a character brings these questions to the foreground, and his preoccupation with the kid—with his behavior and choices—makes ethics and human nature the conceptual field upon which a deadly game of thought and action is enacted. In this way, Judeo-Christian cosmology and typology, scientific materialism with its often purely atheist implications, the continental philosophy of Friedrich Nietzsche, philosophical nihilism, and the fascinating conceptions of ancient Gnosticism, all appear personified in the strange figure of Judge Holden, who is by no means a patchwork creation of competing philosophical configurations, but a distinctive artistic embodiment of darkness that stands apart but nevertheless draws on these various perspectives. These

issues appear also in subjectively rendered descriptions of landscape, rich with symbolic and typological import, as well as in the image patterns of the carnivalesque.

Early in the novel, the kid enters a carnival scene in a town, where a team of dancers parade the street: "They wore strange costumes all, the men in dark flatcrowned hats, white nightshirts, trousers that buttoned up the outside leg and the girls with garish painted faces and tortoiseshell combs in their blue-black hair" (22). In its normative imbalance, the scene suggests the transgression of moral boundaries that will later define the novel through the figure of the judge. In terms of landscape, the desert in its bleakness at times encourages a purely materialist and antireligious conception of nature, and natural process appears as the ruthless band travels through the desert in search of water. Their plight is reflected in all they see, even in the sunrise, and while these descriptions involve no doctrinaire pronouncement of scientific naturalism and materialism, it portrays a stark image of struggle and depravation, suffering and death, reminiscent of many of the works of Stephen Crane and Jack London. "Dryness," "dust," "sand," and "grit" frame the pathetic battle of small things who desperately attempt to live. But McCarthy renders the landscape evocatively, again through the use of surreal imagery and elements of wasteland iconography as well as biblical typology, and in a passage that follows, the treatment of nature takes on a strange sense of mystery and the otherworldly: "All night sheetlightning quaked sourceless to the west beyond the midnight thunderheads, making a bluish day of the distant desert, the mountains on the sudden skyline stark and black and livid like a land of some other order out there whose true geology was not stone but fear" (47). McCarthy describes a natural phenomenon, sheet lightning, one that can be explained

scientifically and is experienced often by those who travel the deserts of the American Southwest. In emphasizing the mysteries of nature, the author doesn't resort to the unexplainable but, like many writers of nineteenth-century romantic fiction, configures nature in figurative terms. Readers are invited to conceptualize beyond the scientific and to ponder the deeper symbolic implications of tactile and sensory experience, since that order is characterized not just by its physical features but is the outer projection of the interior reality of human consciousness in "fear." The passage moves with notable dexterity from the physical to the psychological, the scientific to the philosophical and religious, as a discernible natural event connotes an "order" that is obliquely related but ultimately indiscernible. The natural world defines and constrains, through physical law, all objects, animate and inanimate, that are confined and circumscribed by its indifferent operation and processes. But it is also an elaborate metaphor for an incomprehensible realm that exists beyond human perception and reason.

This fascinating pairing of the scientific and the mystical, this strange blending of apparent opposites, appears in the ruminations of the judge as he speaks an "extemporary lecture" to the gang. As the dark manifestation of Enlightenment science, the judge is the bleak personification of a version of positivism largely unacceptable to those who might argue for a model of scientific inquiry defined by optimistic, even progressivist notions of human improvement. As he speaks of the age of the earth, some of his listeners quote scripture. But he responds in the following dialogue:

Books lie, he said.
God don't lie [a gang member responds]
No, said the judge. He does not. And these are his words.

He held up a chunk of rock.

He speaks in stones and trees, the bones of things. (116)

His response is compelling but ambiguous, suggesting some other and darker version of Emersonian Transcendentalism, or conversely implying a reduced notion of God as metaphor for the laws that govern material nature. The judge turns the words of the gang against themselves and in the end posits a world-centered cosmology, placing himself at the apex, when in the dance scene at the novel's conclusion the narrator notes the judge's confident claim that he will never die. Amid this focus on the natural world, these strange suggestions of the divine exist, evidenced in the reference to God, the notion of an alternative order, and the mysterious idea of man's mirrored destiny in another realm of being. McCarthy continually attempts to blend the tactile and experiential with the mystical and sublime, always with full recognition of the world's indifference and brutality. The judge then presents himself as the supreme manifestation of a force driven by material cause and struggle, but his refined consciousness, so erudite and compelling, is in the end a confluence of will that draws its source from the realm of the unknown. Like the white whale in *Moby-Dick,* he is described as ubiquitous, since in the former priest Tobin's words, "Every man in the company claims to have encountered that sootysouled rascal in some other place" (124).

But the judge's characterization of himself is not simple or easily understood. As he ruminates on the role and purpose of war, he becomes a fascinating blend of the aforementioned antireligious scientific materialism and perhaps the Nietzschean *Übermensch* and either the lesser archons or the demiurge of ancient Gnosticism. Often considered the founder of contemporary continental philosophy, the nineteenth-century

German philosopher Friedrich Nietzsche (1844–1900) is a central figure in a revolutionary reconsideration of the history of philosophical and scientific thought. A rough contemporary of Charles Darwin (1809–1882), Herbert Spencer (1820–1903), and T. H. Huxley (1825–1895), who were major figures of the scientific revolution in biology, Nietzsche shares their sense of the limitations of the Judeo-Christian tradition. But he also rejects the scientific method as a primary means of generating knowledge, arguing for a more radical notion of human freedom through the concept of truth as defined by individual will, desire, and perspective. In works such as *Thus Spoke Zarathustra* and *Beyond Good and Evil*, Nietzsche posits an antireligious and antiscientific notion of truth and morality by asserting, in the absence of transcendent Good configured in absolutist terms, an approach to life and choice governed by human intention. The *Übermensch* or "Superman" defines his own morality and asserts his indomitable will upon the world. In a different historical context, the ancient Gnosticism of the first-century Mediterranean and Middle-Eastern regions emerged from a metaphysical conception that asserts that human souls are trapped in a material world dominated by archons, lesser gods of malevolence and brutality that created man in order to trap and contain elements of divine substance. These archons emerged from a more comprehensive and indefinable force of evil referred to as the "demiurge." Release and an apprehension of the divine Good, which exists outside the material world, are difficult matters and are achieved only through *gnosis*, which is direct experience or knowledge of God. Thus evil becomes the most observable and present metaphysical reality in the physical realm. While he reflects the darker potentialities of Enlightenment positivism, the judge also echoes notions potentially drawn,

perhaps equally, from Nietzsche and Gnostic cosmology.[9] The judge's assertion of pure self-determination and Nietzschean will to power is relatively unambiguous, but his status in the context of Gnosticism is less clear. After he has asked Tobin what the judge is the judge of, the kid has a dream in which he sees a mysterious forger who casts a false coin, which suggests human beings themselves who have been cast by the archons. The forger casts "from cold slag brute a face that will pass . . . as current in the markets where men barter" (310). The coin and by implication the human species are counterfeit currency in the world, a mere collection of husks designed for the malevolent purpose of imprisoning the divine. In his concrete presence in the novel, the judge more often seems to echo the role of the lesser archons, one of many lords of the material world who serve a greater and more mysterious evil. But in the dream he stands behind the forger, "enshadowing" him and presiding over his creative activity. In this sense he suggests something larger and more horrifying—perhaps the demiurge itself.

These complementary intellectual configurations appear in the judge's many monologues, which are informed by nineteenth-century natural philosophy. His language is explicitly philosophical, as he engages questions related to ultimate meaning, purpose, and morality. His varied and complex worldview rejects preconceived notions of moral structure and decency. Any order that exists in the universe is made manifest through the assertion of will upon will, desire upon desire, violence upon violence. McCarthy implies Nietzsche's philosophy of the *Übermensch* and gives it life in the historical figure of Judge Holden, and in doing so explores the implications of the philosopher's elaborate system of ideas. For the judge, the most defining instrument for enacting violence is directed and individual human impulse,

and insofar as that force is where the laws of nature coalesce in their purest form, then in the judge's view, "War is God." The judge states that "war is the truest form of divination. It is the testing of one's will and the will of another within that larger will. . . . War is the ultimate game because war is at last a forcing of the unity of existence. War is God" (249).

Through the judge, McCarthy blends the evolutionary naturalism of the late nineteenth century, with its recognition of the violence in nature and the indifference to human suffering inherent in natural law, with the radically human-centered philosophy of Nietzsche. War and violence are unavoidable characteristics of existence, and order is achieved only through deliberate and forceful acts of violence. Through that destructive impulse the individual human achieves the closest thing to divine status. But the judge's character, his extraordinary intellectual ability as well as his seeming indomitability, make him more than a worldly philosopher of brutish impulse. A different feature of his character appears throughout the novel, but never more dramatically than at the novel's conclusion, when after he has confronted the kid for the last time, he presides over a carnivalesque scene that seems a microcosm of the malevolent world in which human beings live and struggle. This ritual is defined by the "dance," which the judge describes not just as an act but as a state of being that transcends the physical and achieves meaning by acknowledging the primacy of destruction. In his last attempt to convert the kid, the judge claims that "only that man who has offered himself entire to the blood of war . . . and learned at last that it speaks to his inmost heart, only that man can dance" (331). After this interchange and what appears to be the kid's death in the jakes, the judge presides in ritual and reality, claiming his immortality. He emerges here as more than an

extraordinary man, but as part of the defining reality of the material world, the ubiquitous and evil force that orders the violent play of material existence. Whether he is that defining reality in its totality (demiurge) or one of many lesser emanations of that force (archon) remains uncertain, but the general pattern of ancient Near-Eastern Gnosticism seems to echo forcefully in his character.

However, there is a compelling ambiguity built into the judge's expression that centers on the question of whether to take his terminology literally or figuratively, or, to deepen the complexity, to contend with the blending of the literal and the figurative. Critics who have interpreted the text in Gnostic terms have tended to read the judge's use of the word "God" in loosely literal terms, since he ultimately figures himself as the spiritualized force that holds sway over the world and stands between that world and the true light of purity and goodness that exists beyond. In this sense, *demiurge* as "God" is a deity of malevolence and destruction whose argument sustains its power through the compelling logic of force and will, a force that through violence and destruction initiates and maintains the unity of existence. But given that the judge is also the avatar of the Enlightenment, the literary creation of a late-twentieth-century writer fascinated with science and philosophy, his use of the word *God* may be figurative in the same sense that it is used by some modern physicists—Spinoza's God—God as a metaphor for the unity of natural law and cosmological order, impersonal and inhuman, the antithesis of the anthropomorphic God of the Judeo-Christian tradition. In this latter sense, the judge's evocative pronouncement is a rather poetic but direct expression of a scientific materialism that does more than simply deny the existence of God, but does so by appropriating and essentially

redefining the term "God" through a deft act of displacement and reconsideration. In the judge's hands, however, the Enlightenment notion of divine principle as natural law is not benign or morally neutral. It is not the deistic conception of an optimistic and progressive scientific positivism. Instead, it is actively malevolent and destructive. As such, McCarthy places the utopian impulses of scientific materialism under the severe and harsh light of skeptical inquiry.

Thus the formidable figure of Judge Holden, drawn from actual history but reconfigured in McCarthy's imagination as the symbol and expression of evil in all its material, intellectual, and spiritual forms, becomes a dominant voice in the world of *Blood Meridian*. But that voice speaks to a silent but active observer who becomes simultaneously his goal and his adversary. In the course of the novel, the kid says very little, but it is the manner in which he listens and later acts that makes him perhaps an equally dominant force, functioning as a heroic counterbalance to the judge's view of things. The kid is unquestionably a member of the gang, with a proclivity for violence that McCarthy notes on the first page of the novel. Though readers never see him engaging in an act of scalping or murder, his very presence with the gang assumes his complicity. Still, he stands apart, not because of his purity or separation from the judge's world, but because in the end he responds to circumstances with a moral rectitude and resists the judge's pronouncements even unto death. In spite of Judge Holden's verbal and physical power, one of the kid's final statements to him after encountering him many years later is simple and poignant: "You aint nothin" (331). The kid's resistance is implicitly founded on a faith in the transformative power of moral order and meaning, as well as ethics and benevolence, and at the center of these virtues is the question of

God and his nature. There is a striking power in the way in which McCarthy imagines how God becomes incarnate in the world, which is made clear to the kid as he quietly ruminates on the question of the divine. This evolving recognition is brought about by the former priest Tobin. The former priest plays a central and fascinating role in revealing the kid's internal conflict. Clearly of a different ethical frame than the rest of the gang, the kid has many opportunities to kill the murderous judge, an act that would confirm in large part the judge's version of reality. But he does not do so. Still, he remains skeptical of any transcendent purpose or value, at first denying the God that many in the gang, ironically, still hold to be real. In a fascinating exchange, Tobin and the kid reflect on the idea. At first speaking in somewhat conventional terms, the former priest ends with a compelling and philosophically packed claim:

> No man is leave of that voice.
> The kid spat into the fire and bent to his work.
> I aint heard no voice, he said.
> When it stops, said Tobin, you'll know you've heard it
>   all your life. (124)

Here the former priest attempts a strange integration of the natural and the supernatural, especially in the ubiquitous "voice" that is so constant and defining that it cannot be heard except by those who are attuned to its resonance. The priest's apostate status, the fact that he has abandoned his vocation to travel with a murderous band of scalp hunters, suggests that even he is unsure of the moral status of the divine. In his words and responses to those who speak to him, the kid remains relatively quiet. But like many of McCarthy's wandering heroes, he speaks with clarity in his telling moments of silence, in his implicit rejection of the

judge's abhorrent philosophy of violence, and in his basic actions, behaviors that the judge calls out as inconsistent with his own nature. This appears clearly as the kid risks his own life in an attempt to save the life of a wounded comrade, an act antithetical to the judge's and the gang's practice and belief. After they separate and become adversaries, the judge is aware of the many times he has offered the kid the opportunity to kill him. This is surface evidence of other actions that distinguish the kid from the rest of the gang, and the judge emerges in this context as a rather conventional Satan figure intent upon converting his protégé to his worldview and behavior. On the one hand, the judge speaks to the kid with an intensely paternal language, which resonates with religious implications, when in their final interchange the judge says, "Don't you know that I'd have loved you like a son?" (306). From the judge's perspective, the kid is distinctively gifted, and in his mysterious endowments he becomes a chosen figure, both in affection and in mission. But the kid's resistance never wavers, though it is sometimes filled with anxiety and palpable fear. Toward the end of the novel, the gang has been wiped out. Glanton has died, and a few of them have narrowly escaped a massacre by the Yuma Indians. As they flee, the judge remains confident of his own seeming immortality, and when he concludes that the kid is lost to him, he responds with a harsh resolve and studied resignation: "There's a flawed place in the fabric of your heart. . . . You alone were mutinous. You alone reserved in your soul some corner of clemency for the heathen" (299).

In the midst of the novel's darkness and violent intensity, even against the compelling pronouncements of the judge, the kid responds to the silent voice the former priest illuminates in a quiet moment in the wilderness. This voice articulates its mystery

language in resonating echoes in all that can be seen, felt, and intimated by the heart. No man is leave of that voice. But the kid is no ordinary man, since in hearing the voice he responds by staying his own violent hand, even against the heart of transcendent evil itself. This is a fact the judge cannot accept, and in their encounter nearly thirty years later he seemingly has no choice but to kill him. But before he does so, as he explains the strange ritual of the dance, the judge continues to speak in the vain hope the kid will finally relent: "Is not blood the tempering agent in the mortar which bonds?" (329). The kid answers peremptorily, saying, "I don't like craziness" (330), and the judge continues his monologue in a vague justification of malevolence rooted in an obtuse, darkly deterministic, philosophical language. But in the end the kid invites his own death by reducing the judge to "nothing," simply by dismissing him with relative silence. His death then becomes a measured victory that echoes Christ's death on the cross, at least insofar as he is destroyed but never internally defeated, and he stands as an example of moral rectitude and heroism in the face of omnipresent evil. Seemingly, the judge presides in the end—dancing naked among the fiddlers and the prostitutes, near the bear who lies in an immense pool of blood—his bone-white head illuminated palely by the lamps as he claims the inviolability of his presence and all it represents.

It appears then, that in spite of the kid's resistance, the world remains the judge's domain, a place in which heroic resolve and moral rectitude must inevitably end in death. This stark reality remains a real possibility, depending largely on how one reads the conclusion. The novel ends with an evocative and mysterious epilogue that initiates the image of fire, which will reappear again in *No Country for Old Men* and *The Road*. This passage is the novel's last moment of forceful expression, and it has been

associated with Milton's *Lycidas* and identified historically as perhaps Walter De Maria's *Lightning Field*.[10] De Maria's work of minimalist land art was completed in 1977 and is located near Quemado, New Mexico. It consists of four hundred stainless steel poles formed in a grid running one mile by one kilometer and six meters. Christopher D. Campbell notes the striking similarity between the field and the events in the epilogue, linking McCarthy's potential use of the field to Leo Daugherty's Gnostic reading. In this context, the epilogue may be seen as McCarthy's self-portrait of the artist alienated from the killing world (the novel makes reference to Anareta, a planet in Renaissance cosmology that is believed to destroy life). The artist (both De Maria and McCarthy) seeks the light and hope that in Gnostic conception is trapped within the physical world. Harold Bloom views this Gnostic reading as limiting, suggesting that the figure of the judge transcends any one conception of evil. He points to McCarthy's own warning in a passage when the judge is in jail, in which the narrator claims that he cannot be reduced to his origins or confined within any system, heterodox or otherwise. It is perhaps more fruitful to consider that various notions of evil, literary or philosophical, partially illuminate rather than define his nature. In Bloom's view this is what marks his greatness as a character. However, Bloom does concur with Daugherty in seeing the epilogue as a complex image of hope, as an allusion to the myth of Prometheus, a figure in Greek mythology who in defiance of the greater gods gives fire to the human race, and who in the context of *Blood Meridian* perpetually stands in opposition to the judge. The epilogue is a brief italicized vignette, in which an unnamed man is traveling across a plain making holes in a floor of stone with a steel implement, *"striking the fire out of the rock which God has put there"* (337). He is followed

by other wanderers, and they form an unlikely communion of souls—a microcosm of the human community. They move in a manner that "*seems less the pursuit of some continuance than the verification of a principle, a validation of sequence and causality as if each round and perfect hole owed its existence to the one before it*" (337). The dreamlike and surreal quality of the epilogue does little to compromise its measured clarity, following hard upon the judge's dance. The image of fire here is somewhat ambiguous, but in later novels it is a vivid, striking, and evocative intimation of the divine, and with it stands the "principle" of cause, effect, and purpose that makes order of apparent chaos. The man and the gatherers form a disparate community of seekers who create order through fire and in Bloom's view represent the Promethean force that does and will always stand against Judge Holden. It is telling that the novel concludes with a scene that reinforces the kid's final affirmation of benevolence in the context of isolation, which involves a kind of Promethean defiance that leads to his death. Like the wanderers, he lives and dies in the cold desolation of the plain, seemingly alone, but the divine fire finds its expression in human terms in his distinctive nature. This powerful image invites a consideration of the epigraph from Jakob Böhme (1587–1624) that begins the novel.[11] The epigraph reads: "It is not to be thought that the life of darkness is sunk in misery and lost as if in sorrowing. There is no sorrowing. For sorrow is a thing that is swallowed up in death, and death and dying are the very life of the darkness."

Böhme was a Lutheran mystic who, though devout, was considered theologically unorthodox and by some even heretical. In *Die Morgenroete im Aufgang* (1610), *Aurora* (1612), *Weg zu Christo* (1622; *The Way to Christ*), and *Mysterium Magnum*

(1623; *The Great Mystery*), he explored the relationship of the human race to God as a perpetual tension between sin and redemption. Consistent with Christian theology broadly and Lutheran theology specifically, human beings exist in a fallen state, alienated from the divine and dependent upon grace for salvation. But Böhme's notions became controversial insofar as he saw the fall as a necessary stage in the evolution of God's creation. Human beings must fall into the hell that is the material world, and through a mysterious process of purification they may reach the "fire" that is associated with the Father and the "light" that is Christ. This preordained historical process involves a separation from the divine Good and an entrapment in the hellish materiality that is the world, a materiality of suffering that in the end is "swallowed up in death," in the divine fire that marks the redemptive power of God. Though definitively within the Christian tradition, Böhme's conception bears a clear similarity to Gnosticism. The wanderers and the image of the fire in the epilogue might refer to an array of complimentary sources: the Gnosticism of the ancient Near East in the first century C.E., the Greek myth of Prometheus, and the divine fire central to the theology of the post-Reformation Lutheran mystic Jakob Böhme. As with the character of judge, these and perhaps other sources blend into the distinct and evocative imagery of the epilogue. This final passage stands on its own as a mysterious image of future possibility in which the judge does not wholly preside. Still *Blood Meridian* is by no means a forthright affirmation of human heroism and decency, and the rendering of violence, together with the compelling character of Judge Holden, seems at times like an extended nightmare in human language. But neither is it the programmatic expression of nihilism that to some it appears to be, since it closes on a principle or order, expressed in

an image of community, seeking, and the present possibility of clemency, even for those whose souls are compromised by greed, loss, and violence. The novel is perhaps the most notable late-twentieth-century expression of a tradition that draws its roots from Melville and Dostoyevsky, novels that take the human situation as their primary concern, but deepen that condition through an intimate grasp of the interiors of the human heart, seeking answers to the inescapable questions that amid the frenetic activity of human striving lie only half present—yet are part of the defining substance of consciousness itself.

The Border Trilogy

Until the publication of *All the Pretty Horses* in 1992, none of Cormac McCarthy's novels sold more than five thousand copies in hardback. Critical reception was seldom indifferent, and many reviewers considered him one of the finest writers of his generation. Still, it is safe to assume that subsequent to the first novel in the Border Trilogy he survived primarily by frugal living, scant royalties, and revenue from his many grants and fellowships, most notably the coveted MacArthur Genius Grant. After his move to El Paso (in part to research *Blood Meridian*), his novels take the West as subject, and the Border Trilogy may be seen as a meditation on the distinctive historical circumstances of the late twentieth century. The context is the Second World War and its aftermath in the cold war, and the settings are often situated near the nuclear testing grounds of the American southwest. The image that concludes *All the Pretty Horses*—as John Grady Cole rides into the "bloodred sunset," watching a bull writhing like "an animal in sacrificial torment"—is evocative of an atomic explosion.[1] But the history that informs the trilogy forms only the surface texture of a deeply philosophical and portentous story that is deceptively unified. Much like the mythic cowboy figures in other "westerns," John Grady Cole and Billy Parham are quiet men of work, who aspire to the autonomy and freedom that has always been the promise of the frontier experience. But their encounters with the modern world are rife with ethical, moral, and religious implications, and their

most telling actions may be as listeners and initiates, heroes of another order who come to perceive in compelling ways truths and realms that transcend normative experience.

Although when the novel appeared these deeper themes risked alienating broad audiences interested in the western genre, *All the Pretty Horses* became a critical and popular success, emerging as a *New York Times* best seller, selling 190,000 copies in hardcover within the first six months of initial publication. After the retirement of Albert Erskine of Random House, McCarthy hired Amanda Urban as his agent and moved to Alfred A. Knopf under the editorship of Gary Fisketjon, who worked diligently to increase the author's public exposure. Partly as a favor to Erskine, McCarthy granted his first interview to Richard B. Woodward of the *New York Times Magazine*. Entitled "McCarthy's Venomous Fiction," this congenial interchange offers glimpses into the author's philosophical and scientific interests, aesthetic concerns, even some of his greatest influences, which of course include Melville, Dostoyevsky, and Faulkner. Always reluctant to discuss his work directly, McCarthy nevertheless ponders the nature of violence, which seems endemic to the physical world, musing alternatively on the physiology of Mojave rattlesnakes and the essential themes of what he considers the most important works of literary art. Knopf released *The Crossing* in 1994 with an initial printing of 200,000 copies followed by a second printing of 25,000 that occurred within a month of the initial run. The trilogy concludes in 1998 with *Cities of the Plain*, a novel that unites the protagonists of the first two novels. In terms of conception and execution, *Cities of the Plain* begins the trilogy since it started as a film script, which McCarthy wrote sometime in the 1980s.[2] After unsuccessful attempts to place the screenplay, he reenvisoned the story in

novel form, though he may have intended to do so all along. According to Gary Fisketjon, the author first planned to write only two novels with John Grady Cole as the primary character, but as McCarthy conceptualized the broader story, Billy Parham became an important figure, and *The Crossing* emerged as the most densely complex volume in the trilogy, rivaling *Blood Meridian* in its philosophical intensity. McCarthy's move to the West and the transition in setting that occurs with *Blood Meridian* marks a shift in more than locale, as the western novels involve a distinctive blending of popular and literary aesthetics and genre conventions, ornate and minimalist language, and a deepening of philosophical and religious concerns. Some consider *Blood Meridian* and the Border Trilogy his greatest works, but it remains for readers and critics to categorize and evaluate which period in the author's career is most important and for what reasons. But in bringing McCarthy into public consciousness, the Border Trilogy displays no perceivable artistic compromise, since the novels explore the role of history, myth, dreams, and human community and friendship in the dense and compelling context of the modern moment.

All the Pretty Horses (1992)

In *All the Pretty Horses,* McCarthy retains his stark vision of blood and reverence, unremitting despair and stoic resolve, human dilemma and silent action. But this first novel in the Border Trilogy, especially when considered in the context of *Blood Meridian,* involves a softening of perspective, with a deeper, more moderate tone and a clearer sense of hope and possibility, even as it charts the destruction of the old social order and confronts the inexorable forces of the postnuclear world. In the decade following its publication, the responses of academic

critics have been respectful, largely positive if somewhat varied. But reviews in the popular magazines were most commonly laudatory. The novel won both the National Book Award and the National Book Critics Circle Award, and film rights were quickly optioned by Columbia Pictures, resulting in a feature-length production released in 2000, directed by Billy Bob Thornton.[3]

An understandable inertia followed these accolades, resulting in McCarthy's first best seller and wide critical attention that was notably lacking after the publication of *Blood Meridian.* Reviews of *All the Pretty Horses,* though often passionately enthusiastic, were nonetheless detailed and nuanced. What is perhaps most remarkable about them is how they depart from previous treatments. Faulkner is mentioned yet again, but critics more often point to McCarthy's departure from his predecessor in the southern tradition. An anonymous reviewer in the *New Yorker* makes reference to Faulkner only indirectly, writing that "in the hands of a lesser talent, the Faulknerian prose . . . would have become stylized and sepia-toned, but right from the start Mr. McCarthy brings great imaginative competence and conviction to the tale."[4] The author's language and stylistic skill remain things to be admired, but Faulkner becomes more a figure of effective comparison, rather than an oppressive shadow muting the original force of McCarthy's vision. In the *New York Times Book Review,* Madison Smartt Bell comments on the "extraordinary quality of his prose," which is best described as "overwhelmingly seductive" in its varied use of erudition, lyricism, and realistic dialogue. But it stands on its own merits, since the author "builds on Faulkner's work yet, more than Faulkner ever did . . . seems to be pulling the language apart at its roots," evoking "Elizabethan language in its flux of remarkable possibilities."[5] Critics seem unwilling and perhaps unable to comment

on McCarthy's novels without references to the most notable works in the Western literary tradition, further reinforcing the author's unselfconscious confession that books are made from other books. But in these reviews the suspicion of excessive influence largely disappears. In the *Chicago Tribune,* Christopher Zenowich sees the protagonist John Grady Cole as "a post-war American Ishmael, disenfranchised by his family but in search of something that goes beyond mere property." He refers to the novel as "a prayer in prose fiction" and "a homage to the world," concluding finally that readers will inevitably be moved by the singular force of imagination reflected in the novel: "It's time we looked at ourselves through the vision of Cormac McCarthy."[6] In all this, however, there was some dissent. In the *Times Literary Supplement,* with condescending sympathy John Sutherland compares the novel to popular westerns such as those of Zane Grey, Jack Schaefer, and J. T. Hudson, with no mention of one of McCarthy's most recent favorites, Larry McMurtry's Pulitzer Prize–winning *Lonesome Dove.*[7] In pointing to parallels in setting and historical context, Sutherland twice places *All the Pretty Horses* alongside Peter Bogdanovich's *The Last Picture Show,* apparently unaware that the film was an adaptation of McMurtry's critically acclaimed novel of the same name. A troubling anti-American bias and a tendency to stereotype appear in Sutherland's treatment of McCarthy's style, which is characterized as "laconic and artfully lazy, like the speech of the region."[8] Sutherland's criticism becomes more substantive as he ponders what he sees as ineffective characterization, claiming that "John Grady Cole remains a rather insubstantial creation."[9] Still this overarching treatment of the novel as yet another American western evoked a passionate response from readers in a number of letters to the editor. Douglas Cooper, a Canadian reader

living in New York, writes that "a careful review might have searched for sources and symbols somewhere other than Peckinpah," pondering further Sutherland's British bias, saying that "it is hardly going to impress him to note complex allegorical tendencies; which makes me wonder: what would impress him? Perhaps something a little less American?"[10] Also of New York, Daniel Conaway expresses similar concerns, writing that Sutherland's review "rings the same dull refrain English critics have been sounding since the days of Whitman and Emerson."[11] Sutherland's assessment and the American and Canadian responses are interesting insofar as they reveal a tendency both to summarily characterize and vigorously defend the western genre, and this tension is by no means merely a cross-continental phenomenon. The popularity of *All the Pretty Horses,* the fact that it is the first work that brings the author fully into the public view, certainly emerges from the fact that it is a modern western replete with the conventions of nostalgic romance, with elegiac rhythms of language that gain strength from idyllic images of wild horses and the young men taming and riding them. But the consensus that emerges is that the novel enlivens and enriches a genre that is deceptively rich in the first place. In the *Village Voice,* Michael Coffey betrays a mixed sympathy to the western while extolling the virtues of McCarthy's novel: "When their adolescence pokes through the cowboy veneer, the book takes on an almost quixotic feel" in prose that "puts it on the line at full gallop, unafraid to fail or fall."[12] In his second book in the western period and the first in the Border Trilogy, McCarthy retains his bleak vision, continues yet alters his lyrical style, and lifts a popular form into the realm of the literary. He engages questions of personal identity, nature, and modernity, all in the context of his continual pursuit of meaning amid concerns both human and divine.

The novel is set in 1949, exactly one hundred years after *Blood Meridian*'s the kid confronts Judge Holden in Nacogdoches. The same issues resonate in the experiences of the protagonists: the search for self in a violent world, the confrontation with evil, the embodied mystical quality of nature, the effects of time and historical change, and the question of God's existence and purpose in a universe that draws its essence from mystery. But as well as being a western, *All the Pretty Horses* is also a bildungsroman, a coming-of-age story told using the most popular genre in American literature and film. John Grady Cole is the sixteen-year-old descendant of a long line of Texas cattlemen, the maternal grandson of a rancher who owned a large piece of land near San Angelo. His grandfather has died, his parents have divorced, and his mother has decided to sell the ranch to a Texas oil company. But John Grady is a consummate horseman with a mystic's sense of the animal's nature, an intimate grasp of its relation to mysterious realms that transcend. After realizing the land is lost to him, he sets out with his friend Lacey Rawlins to seek the older, premodern social order in Mexico. They travel on horseback across the border, tying their horses at gas stations, eating in cafes, hunting on the mesquite plains and arroyos of northern Mexico, and descriptions of their journey involve a strange blend of old and new: highways and cattle ranches; cafes and campfires, oil derricks and ancient traces cut by the Comanche; even pristine natural sunsets and blood-red skies, the latter made so perhaps by the nuclear tests conducted in the Southwest after the war. The young men soon encounter a bereft fourteen-year-old runaway named Jimmy Blevins, who is riding a stolen horse, and as they reluctantly take him in they are caught in a web of legal difficulty. Separating from Blevins and narrowly escaping the law, they find themselves working as ranch hands on a vast estate owned by Don Héctor Rocha y

Villarreal, known as the Hacienda de Nuestra Señora de la Purísima Concepcíon. John Grady Cole's gift with horses is soon recognized as he finds himself a favorite and a confidant of Don Héctor, but he also becomes involved in a passionate affair with the rancher's daughter, Alejandra, who is the charge of Dueña Alfonsa, the wise but jaded matriarch of the old aristocratic family. A complex interchange ensues and John Grady Cole and Lacey Rawlins find themselves imprisoned in Saltillo, where they must survive amid the violence and savagery that reign beneath a thin veneer of civilization and decorum. In the context of this experience, John Grady comes to manhood as he confronts his own potential for violent action and struggles to make sense of a world defined by love and malevolence, friendship and betrayal, ethics and their antithesis in personal desire. A contemporary frontier romance with mythic resonance, *All the Pretty Horses* charts the slow tragedy of historical change, while engaging questions of personal responsibility in the context of a world of light and shadow.

The novel is often characterized as more accessible than McCarthy's previous works, partly because of its structure and mainly since it evokes the conventions of the western epic romance. Still, *All the Pretty Horses* presents unique challenges, and it is by no means standard fare for readers of popular westerns. From the very beginning, the density of the prose both repels and attracts, depending upon the varying sensibilities of those who encounter it. The first sentence anticipates patterns of ornate imagery that are a common feature of the novel's formal texture: "The candleflame and the image of the candleflame caught in the pierglass twisted and righted when he entered the hall and again when he shut the door" (3). The unconventional compounding of "candle" and "flame" notwithstanding, the

image captures both the fire itself and its distorted reflection, together with its changing shape in response to natural forces. The passage is rich and evocative but requires attention to detail since it initiates the dream motif that will become an essential element of the protagonist's character. At certain points, dialogue is presented in Spanish, creating a sense of immediacy and realism. Generally, however, the major interchanges that carry the most essential thematic content are conducted in English. Overall, the novel's narrative line is conventional enough, with a picaresque quality organized loosely around a journey narrative, which is often typical of the bildungsroman or coming-of-age story. But there are no chapter breaks. Instead, the book is divided into four long parts that are not designated as such, but are titled in Roman numerals with few section breaks between paragraphs, making it difficult for readers to find places to pause. The novel is best read at leisure over extended periods of time. The first section charts John Grady's decision to leave Texas, his journey across the border with Rawlins, and their troubling escapades with Jimmy Blevins. The second recounts the three months John Grady and Rawlins spend at Hacienda de Nuestra Señora de la Purísima Concepcíon, centering on John Grady's passionate affair with Alejandra. The third involves the brutal experiences of their arrest and interrogation by the captain in Encantada, the murder of Blevins, and the time spent defending themselves against the horrors of the prison in Saltillo. The fourth is the most extensive, recounting their release from prison, the long conversation with Dueña Alfonsa, John Grady's final encounter with Alejandra, his rescue of the horses from the captain, and finally his return to Texas.

These extended sequences have the purposeful effect of giving the novel a surreal quality, and McCarthy is not subtle in his use

of the dream motif, since this mode of perception becomes a defining feature of John Grady's character and consciousness, his particular brand of modern heroism.[13] As he comes to a tentative grasp of his place in the world, the essential tension for John Grady involves the dissonance between his interior conceptions, in essence his dreams, whether literal or figurative, and the reality of the circumstances he confronts in a normative state of tactile awareness. This tension involves the mental distances that separate past and present, that distinguish the idyllic world of ranches and horses from oil companies, banks, and ubiquitous corporate interests. It also portrays the differing conceptions of nature and its meaning as figured in the image of the horse. The novel's title is drawn from an Appalachian folksong of the same name that emerges from a varied oral tradition. In one version, it is a lullaby sung by a grandmother, as she sweetly conjures the image of the "pretty horses" she hopes will imbue the child's dreams with a sense of comfort and repose. In spite of his stoic resolve, John Grady is just this child. After his arrest, as he lies on the dirt floor of the jail in Encantada, he sleeps. And in that sleep he dreams: "That night he dreamt of horses in a field on a high plain where the spring rains had brought up the grass and the wildflowers . . . and they moved all of them in a resonance that was like a music among them and they were none of them afraid . . . and they ran in that resonance which is the world itself and which cannot be spoken but only praised" (162).

Amid the bleak shadows of the prison cell when all is silent, after the loss of his ranch, the harsh betrayal of Don Héctor, and the foolish obstinacy of Blevins, John Grady dreams of horses and wildflowers. The dream resonates in his mind blending with his conscious thoughts, and in a strange alchemy of experience and mental figuration it forms his essential identity, which

increasingly draws strength from the idea that the world is a confluence of the real and the unreal, the tactile and the imaginary, what is and what can be. It is informed by the essential truth of a "resonating" hope that must inspire only praise. But the nature of John Grady's dream-self is by no means purely idyllic, nor does it rise into existence only in the interior realm of sleep. Early in the novel as he quietly laments the sale of the land, he rides alone onto the plain and conjures the past in an imaginary conception of the old Comanche road that traversed a path between the north and middle forks of the Concho River, where "that lost nation came down out of the north with their faces chalked," with "their long hair plaited," as they traveled the trace "armed for war" (5). He sees them in his mind and ponders their place in time, as they ride "nation and ghost nation passing in a soft chorale across that mineral waste to darkness bearing lost to all history and all remembrance like a grail the sum of their secular and transitory and violent lives" (5). John Grady's ability to imagine the horse and the Comanche in order to sustain himself against the reality of his experiences does not involve even a momentary denial of violence and brutality, nor does it imply permanence or stability in place or region. The Comanche are "violent," "transitory," and "secular." The horses are wild, with a strength that mirrors the brutish force of nature itself. But whether conscious or unconscious, these dreams are filled with a sense of mystery and the sublime, and they embody in their evocative power the implication, always omnipresent in McCarthy's novels, that there exists an "other order," an organizing principle of causality inaccessible to human reason, one that stands within and against the apparent disorder of the material world. John Grady returns to these dreams during his moments of greatest struggle, and from them

he derives his stoic resolve, as well as the ethical code that defines him as a modern hero in the making.[14]

In this sense it is through the act of dreaming that John Grady Cole attempts to ordain his future, and while he works for Don Héctor the substance of that future becomes personified in Alejandra. In the extended conversation between John Grady and Dueña Alfonsa, after his release from prison, McCarthy deepens the thematic texture of the novel and explores the relationship between hope and the shaping reality of forces beyond the self. The interchange is largely a monologue in which the old woman explains her opposition to his relationship with Alejandra. Dueña Alfonsa's character and the nature of her expression reflect the influence of Dostoyevsky's *The Brothers Karamazov*, since she emerges as a kind of Grand Inquisitor figure. Like many of McCarthy's philosopher mystics, she speaks at length to a largely silent listener. But her philosophical position is of a different order than that of the Grand Inquisitor, as McCarthy uses her to explore other issues, in this case the roles of fate, individual choice, and human action on the course of history. Hers is a harsh and unforgiving worldview, one that speaks incisively to John Grady's nature and his interior reflections: "The world is quite ruthless in selecting between the dream and the reality, even where we will not" (238). What seems on the surface to be a simple defeatism, an old woman's belief that the ideals of youth are rarely realized, is in fact a more layered and mysterious reflection on the nature of history and self-determination, as well as on the human capacity to know the world and control it. Dueña Alfonsa expresses these concerns in rather lyrical terms, saying, "Between the wish and the thing the world lies waiting. I've thought a great deal about my life and about my country. I think there is little that can be truly known" (238).

This claim is the culmination of an extended rumination on her own life in the context of the history of twentieth-century Mexico. She has been the confidant of Gustavo Madero, the brother of the ill-fated Francisco Madero, who was a fervent intellectual, a revolutionary, and a short-lived Mexican president from 1911 to 1913. Francisco Madero and Dueña Alfonsa shared much in common. The former was an emancipated cultural hybrid, educated in Europe, conditioned in the principles of democratic socialism. He was an aristocrat who was strongly influenced by Marxist social philosophy and modern principles of egalitarian democracy, and he returned to his own country committed to labor reform among industrial workers and to land reform among the agrarian classes. His revolution succeeded in the short term, and he was elected president in 1911. But social divisions and the politics of faction led to his assassination and the failure of his reforms. In her youth, Dueña Alfonsa shared these idealistic sentiments, even to the point of rebellion against the will of her father. But her experience of their dissolution has resulted in a lifetime of reflection on the nature of human will and its effect upon the world. Recalling her father's contemplation of these same issues, she introduces the metaphor of the coin toss (which will be a central device for McCarthy later in No Country for Old Men). But here she focuses on the figure of the coiner himself, who forges the coin from a slug in a tray, and in doing so chooses between one of two images that will be cast on the face of the coin.[15] In No Country for Old Men, the vicious Anton Chigurh invites his victims to "call it," and their lives depend entirely on how the coin lands. For him, the coin has been traveling to the current moment from the instant it was cast. But in All the Pretty Horses, the coin toss that determines fate is initiated by the

coiner, a simple working man who comprehends nothing of the gravity of his actions, though in choosing a face for the coin he may dictate life or death in a complex and unpredictable sequence of cause and effect. In one sense, however, Dueña Alfonsa's father has "a great sense of the connectedness of things" (230), one that she does not entirely concede to, preferring to figure time and its passing in different and even more frightening terms: "For me the world has always been more of a puppet show. But when one looks behind the curtain and traces the strings upward he finds they terminate in the hands of yet other puppets" (231). In both metaphors the origin and the effect of individual choice become utterly unknowable—yet full of consequence. In a paradoxical sense, human beings exert a tremendous influence on the world, but they are powerless to control the process by which their actions bear fruit. Dueña Alfonsa's story of the Madero brothers becomes a grave reflection on the consequences of idealism, which holds fast to the notion of possibility and hope derived from a faith in the human capacity to consciously ordain the history of the world.[16] She rebels against John Grady's commitment to his own dream of a future with Alejandra, primarily because his faith is so strong, and her rejection of him hinges more fully on an indirect sense that he is ill-fated and lost.

As he attempts to explain his relationship to Blevins and his indirect role in the events that led to Blevins's killing of the Mexican official, Dueña Alfonsa acknowledges both his innocence and his guilt, figured in the light of her conception of the world. She is not merely a traditional aristocrat protecting her niece from the suit of a poor foreigner. The past that she has told him of suggests sympathies quite the contrary. But she will not permit Alejandra to become involved with a man whose destiny is

enmeshed in the dark trajectory of the coin toss and the puppet show, one who is in a strange way guilty only because he seems fated to strife. In John Grady's force of will she sees a stubborn pride bereft of wisdom. He is in that sense "that myopic coiner at the press . . . bent jealously at [his] work, determined that not even chaos be outside [his] own making" (241). In a bleak deterministic universe in which human intentions are blighted by forces beyond understanding, she has no sympathy for those especially cursed by the proverbial fates.

Though Dueña Alfonsa speaks with the same intensity as the Grand Inquisitor, her perspective by no means dominates the novel, and like many of McCarthy's protagonists John Grady articulates himself in the equally resounding language of action. His heroism and stoic resolve begin early and inform the narrative to the last page. Even as his hopes are thwarted, his commitment to Blevins and loyalty to Rawlins are beyond common measure, and they stand against the dark ruminations of Dueña Alfonsa. The potential for heroism in the modern industrial postnuclear world is in this sense the primary subject of the novel. Of course the western, reconfigured and made contemporary in *All the Pretty Horses,* is an ideal genre to explore questions of personal identity, courage, and commitment. John Grady displays a physical strength and ability common to most conventional heroes, but his true merit emerges from his rich interiority, his reflection on hope and possibility, especially as it relates to the world at large. At the beginning of section 4, just after his release from prison and before he returns to Don Héctor's ranch, he meets a group of farmworkers. They gather for quiet conversation and share cigarettes, and after a brief encounter John Grady reflects upon his relationship to the human community, considering the "smiles" of the farmworkers, the "good will

which provoked them," which had the "power to protect and confer honor," to "heal men and bring them to safety long after all other resources were exhausted" (219). This touching conclusion regarding the value of human connection comes immediately after he has witnessed the murder of Blevins and the hellish violence of the prison in Saltillo. It is a remarkable revelation given the gravity of his experience; yet through force of will and depth of conscience, he is able to resolve in personal terms the paradox of a world defined by life and death, murder and benevolence.

This complexity of character emerges from an intensely mystical sense of purpose and order that McCarthy has dealt with in many of his previous works, one that becomes a central preoccupation in the other novels of the Border Trilogy and in later works as well. The question of how human beings come to understand their world achieves only a tentative but compelling response in the sublime image of the horse. Again, in a dream that is more real than the world he encounters in a waking state, John Grady apprehends in the horse that principle of purpose seen in the epilogue of *Blood Meridian*: "Finally what he saw in his dream was that the order in the horse's heart was more durable for it was written in a place where no rain could erase it" (280). He has worked with horses all his life—tamed and ridden them, harnessed and worked them—such is the nature of things in a harsh world. But even in this relationship of dominance John Grady establishes an intimacy based upon the mystical apprehension of unity, order, and value embodied in the horse, and his understanding of this reality becomes clearest in his dreams. It is by no means an order of kindness and beneficence alone, since in the end John Grady, even in his acknowledgment of mystery, comes to believe that "the world's heart

beat at some terrible cost" in a relationship of "divergent equity," and that "the blood of multitudes might ultimately be exacted for the vision of a single flower" (282). But in this starkly naturalistic reflection, beauty itself is created and sustained by the wrenching destruction that occurs as life confronts life. From this revelation emerges a vague understanding of the paradox of blood and reverence, as violence begets the sublime image of the flower, which in the end transcends its own material existence in beauty.

Although the novel forces recognition of the omnipresent power of destruction, predicating the hero's stature upon his understanding of this mysterious conspiracy of opposites, McCarthy resolves the story on a principle of value that is by no means strictly scientific or philosophical. This notion of transcendent purpose finds its most poignant expression in tangibly human terms, as John Grady seeks to live by a strict and definable code of ethics. Even after he has survived his ordeal, his conflict is not over. This appears in his final conversation with the Texas judge who presides over the case of the stolen horse. But it begins earlier in the novel, as he explores one of the most important questions posed in McCarthy's works: the question of God's existence and nature, his presence in the world, and his role in steering the course of human lives and world history. After their separation from Blevins and just before they arrive at Don Héctor's hacienda, John Grady and Lacey Rawlins sit talking around a fire, pondering the people they have known as well as their experience in Mexico. Rawlins wonders if there is some unseen yet guiding influence that protects them. He asks the question directly: "You think God looks out for people?" John Grady's response is simple and pointed. He acknowledges both human and natural evil as well as the divine presence that stands

against them. He says: "I'd say He's just about got to. I don't believe we'd make it a day otherwise" (92). Even at a young age, John Grady defines his relationship to the world through a well-moderated paradox. Human beings are deeply flawed, with a tendency to intellectual blindness and greed, malice, and over-weening self-indulgence. They are subject to unknowable forces that narrowly circumscribe their fates. But a divine presence intercedes on their behalf and saves them from themselves. It is only through the intervention of this presence that any near or long-term survival becomes possible. In his brief response to a weighty question, John Grady balances the reality of a harshly deterministic world with notions of purpose, meaning, and value made real through a mysterious yet paternal force, one that for lack of a more definitive term he must call God.

It is this tentative recognition of transcendence that separates him as an ethical being from the many characters he encounters during his journey: the Mexican captain who encourages him to lie about Blevins to save himself; Perez, the leader of the inmates, who claims that Americans are naive because they hold fast to such impractical ideas as the "good" and the "bad"; and even Dueña Alfonsa, who concedes perhaps too readily to the morally neutral forces of fate and destiny. John Grady is committed to a world protected by God, and he sees himself playing a humble but essential role in an ongoing creation. This becomes clear in his protection of Blevins, his friendship with Rawlins, his deep devotion to nature as seen in his relationship with horses. When he is forced to kill a boy in prison and feels the impulse to kill the captain, he is tortured with guilt. The Texas judge praises him for his courage and devotion, in essence lifting him above common humanity, but John Grady is resistant. He visits the judge at night and tells him of his experience in prison, and with

regard to the captain he admits to intense feelings of hatred and malevolence. The judge tries to comfort him, suggesting that he is too hard on himself, but John Grady is firm, saying: "It just bothered me that you might think I was somethin special. I aint" (293). John Grady's heroism is derived from his unwillingness to be defined as such, from his belief that his choices, though they seem uncommon and virtuous, are nothing more than the expression of every man's obligation to act within an elaborate matrix of cause and effect, one that in the end reveals itself in sublime order—the beautiful tapestry that is the world. In this recognition, there is an assent to the truth of the coin toss and the puppet show, insofar as the outcome of human behavior is unpredictable and immeasurable in its sweeping scope. But in the end, individuals can respond to others with justice and decency. The novel concludes as John Grady, after reuniting with Rawlins and returning his horse, rides into a sunset: "The blood-red dust blew down out of the sun" and "horse and rider and horse passed on. . . . Passed and paled into the darkening land, the world to come" (302). The image is evocative and its potential significance is easily missed. It is 1949 and the American West is changing. Cattle ranches give way to oil fields and highways bury the ancient traces of the Comanche. The red of the sky may simply be the sunset, but it may work figuratively as the most stunning symbol of the cold war—the atmospheric burn of the atomic test. In this postnuclear world, human behavior becomes an issue of tremendous gravity, and the moderated heroism of John Grady Cole is the soul of a modern mythology. This new narrative is informed by a code of living born of humility and obligation, emerging from an understanding of a basic truth—that human behavior has consequence, even amid the unknowable densities of an unfathomable world.

The Crossing (1994)

All the Pretty Horses propelled McCarthy into the public consciousness in a deceptively intricate rendering of the conventional western. But subsequently, The Crossing tended to confound expectations with its philosophical density and tortured religious preoccupation. In comparison to the first novel in the Border Trilogy, The Crossing initially sold quite well but sales tapered quickly, perhaps because its pacing and narrative voice appeared reminiscent of earlier works, and partly because, unlike most sequels, the novel introduces an entirely different cast of characters. The heroes of All the Pretty Horses and The Crossing would not meet until Cities of the Plain. Of course, this was the plan all along, since Cities of the Plain was the first work conceptualized in the form of a screenplay that has yet to be produced. In spite of the scant attention from the reading public, reviews of The Crossing were often quite enthusiastic, and critics seemed less perplexed with McCarthy's abstract themes and densely philosophical influences than in the past. Those who considered the whole of McCarthy's work in the context of The Crossing came to apprehend more fully the philosophical and religious subtexts present in his striking visual style. In the New Republic, Sven Birkerts notes that "McCarthy is writing entirely against the grain of our times, against the haste and distraction and the moral diffusion." Birkerts observes more than previous critics that the author "has been, from the start, a writer with strong spiritual leanings." In considering both the southern and the western works, Birkerts charts a path of thematic concern, arguing that "in the early books we heed his exacerbated awareness of violence and cruelty, of evil, without finding much place for the good. But now, in these most recent books, we meet up quite often with decency."[17] The presence of moral order had

been an aspect of McCarthy's world since *The Orchard Keeper,* and it is evident in works as bleak as *Child of God* and *Blood Meridian,* but critics of *All the Pretty Horses* and *The Crossing* place greater emphasis on the redemptive possibilities that emerge from events and the interaction of characters with the world. Reviewers remained enraptured with McCarthy's language and were still quite forthright in acknowledging his influences, but they claimed for him an individual stature distinct from those influences. In the *New York Times Book Review,* Robert Hass calls *The Crossing* "a miracle in prose" that "deserves to sit on the shelf certainly with 'Beloved' and 'As I Lay Dying,' 'Pudd'nhead Wilson' and 'The Confidence-Man.'" He continues to compare McCarthy with writers as significant and varied as William Shakespeare, Samuel Beckett, Miguel de Cervantes, Joseph Conrad, and Ernest Hemingway. For Hass, McCarthy also warrants comparison to filmmakers like John Ford, Sam Peckinpah, and Sergio Leone, as well as Luis Buñuel and Federico Fellini. By noting these influences, Hass by no means diminishes McCarthy's value as an artist, but instead argues that "Mr. McCarthy is a writer who can plunder almost any source and make it his own."[18] In the *Boston Globe,* Gail Caldwell continues with parallels of this sort, writing, "Were the darkest of Scriptures to be flung across America's southern wilds, surely Cormac McCarthy would be their bruised and clear-eyed prophet" since "His is a world where dawn aches with preordained golden sorrow." Like Hass, Caldwell places McCarthy in the context of the canonical authors of world literature, both ancient and modern, and in doing so she affirms the religious and quasi-religious implications of *The Crossing,* noting "the shadowy religiosity of both Flannery O'Connor and Graham Greene," which involves an imaginative realm where

"Nature [is] cruel and swift as a heartbeat, but now God—or at least the idea of God [is] somewhere in the area."[19] It is remarkable that after nearly thirty years of writing novels with titles like *Outer Dark* and *Child of God* critics have been so reticent to note the God question in McCarthy's work, but until *The Crossing* consideration of this issue by reviewers was muted at best. Caldwell cannot escape the author's religious sensibility even in her own critical language, claiming, "In a world of blood and dirt and bone, the written word is Billy's frankincense and myrrh."[20] As had been the case in the past, English reviewers were somewhat less impressed, at times echoing the consistent minority that considered McCarthy's style overwrought and his plots implausible. In the *London Review of Books,* Michael Wood argues that "one of the chief problems in the world of *The Crossing* . . . is that you can't go anywhere without stumbling into some sage or other out to tell you a story." He is somewhat moderate in his judgment of these sequences, writing that "not everything these people say is negligible or bogus." But he does claim that these characters sometimes disrupt the tenor and tone of the novel, since they "eat into the idea of silence and solitude."[21] This reaction is understandable given the lengthy monologues of characters that at first seem ancillary, but these passages are reminiscent of Ivan and the Grand Inquisitor in Dostoyevsky's *The Brother's Karamazov* and Ishmael in Melville's *Moby-Dick,* and they are an important aspect of McCarthy's romance aesthetic, a pattern of expression that pits multiple perspectives in dialogue in an attempt to render a complexity of ideas in a human context. As the second novel in the Border Trilogy, *The Crossing* retains elements of idyll and romance, in its sweeping desert scenes and images of young men traversing the land on horseback, crossing borders both

geographical and spiritual as they emerge into manhood. But the novel deepens these essential concerns, with an intensity drawn from the author's pressing interest in religion and philosophy, as well as a fascination with the subsuming force of stories and their impact on human lives.

The novel begins roughly a decade before the events in *All the Pretty Horses,* and though it is unstated, the threat of world war looms, infusing the narrative with a vague sense of unspeakable dread. The main character is sixteen-year-old Billy Parham, who lives with his parents and his fourteen-year-old brother, Boyd, on a ranch in southern New Mexico. The livestock on the ranch have been raided by a pregnant she-wolf who has risen specter-like from the mountain regions of northern Mexico. Billy leaves home to hunt the animal that he reveres as a mystic symbol of spiritualized nature. He captures the wolf and commits himself to taking her back to Mexico. Descriptions of the she-wolf—its shape, the set and glow of its eyes, its force of will even at the point of death—bring to mind the bear in Faulkner's story of the same name and the great white whale in *Moby-Dick.* The animal is a living creature central to the story's plot and a symbol of rich thematic import, suggesting nature itself in all its beauty and savagery and the principle of divine agency that even in death lives on in dreams. On his journey, Billy refuses numerous offers to sell the wolf, but his intentions are thwarted when he is detained by Mexican authorities. Billy is held for a time and upon his release he finds the wolf imprisoned as a part of a carnival circus where she is baited and brutalized. Attuned to the she-wolf's value as a creature of nature, Billy risks his own safety and kills the animal rather than see her debased. After burying the wolf, he returns home to find his parents murdered, most probably by an Indian he met at the beginning of the novel. He

recovers his brother, Boyd, from a neighbor's house and the two boys undertake another crossing into Mexico in order to recover their horses. In the course of their travels they encounter again the beauty and brute reality of the natural world, as well as the mixed blessing inherent in any interchange with human beings. Through a series of circumstances for the most part beyond Billy's control, the two brothers are separated, as Boyd falls in love with a Mexican girl and secretly leaves. Billy returns to the United States and attempts to join the army to fight in the war but is refused because of a heart condition. He ventures on a third crossing into Mexico in search of Boyd only to find that he has been killed, and the novel reaches a dramatic crescendo with Billy recovering his brother's remains and with firm resolve setting out to bring him home. In three crossings, Billy comes of age through a series of confrontations with incarnate evil and a set of encounters with people who have been tempered by experience. They stand ready to tell him their stories, and from them he gains provisional wisdom as he comes to apprehend, at least vaguely, that he is a player in a universal drama, a single story written by a silent author, who pens the trajectory of single lives with sublime vision and insight beyond human comprehension.

The potential difficulty presented to readers of *The Crossing* has as much to do with expectations as it does with the complexity of language and conceptual depth. On the surface, the novel is a quest narrative promising the romance and adventure typical of the picaresque tradition. The novel delivers in this regard, but these plot motifs work primarily as frameworks for deeper thematic concerns. *The Crossing* is comprised of four parts, three of which coincide with Billy's journeys into Mexico. Part 1 deals with his encounter with the she-wolf and his failed attempt to take her home. Part 2 chronicles his return to New Mexico,

his reunion with Boyd, and their quest to recover the stolen horses. Part 3 recounts their experiences in Mexico, centering especially on the conflict with the one-armed ranch chief and Boyd's romance with the Mexican girl. Finally, Part 4 details Billy's return to the United States and his final attempt to find his brother. Intricately blended with these crossings are the extended monologues of a number of important figures Billy encounters along the way, three of which are of primary importance. These mysterious characters take Billy to the heart of the matter, forcing him to ponder the essential meaning in his experience. Billy silently listens to the priest at Huisiachepic and his tale of the pensioner, to the blind revolutionary and his wife, and to the *gitano,* the gypsy in charge of the wrecked airplane, all who present stories that emerge as original versions of the same condition, the one story, the single narrative of human destiny that subsumes all in its sweeping march toward an ultimate but as yet unknowable purpose. In this sense, *The Crossing* rivals *Blood Meridian,* since it is Melvillean in scope and philosophical complexity, exploring the most essential questions: the role of suffering in the material world, and the possibility and present potential of the divine.

In the broadest sense, the novel employs the formal features of the American historical romance through a character distinctly human but configured as mythic through his heroic action and his tragic encounter with a changing world. A landscape imbued with sublime resonance—even as it passes into memory, violence—and the embodied spirit of nature are all features of the romance tradition in the hands of authors as varied as James Fenimore Cooper, William Gilmore Simms, Herman Melville, William Faulkner, and even (in spite of his objections) Mark Twain.[22] Like John Grady Cole, Billy Parham is motivated by an

uncommon ethical impulse that enriches his character and defines him as a modern hero in the making. Some critics have noted that main characters in McCarthy's works are rarely given voice, since the third-person narrator is omniscient and firmly objective. For some, this leads to novels rich in language and idea and thin in human texture. But what is often missed in these considerations is the distinctive manner in which characters are made round and dynamic, embodied in human terms.[23] John Wesley Rattner, Culla Holme, Lester Ballard, Cornelius Suttree, the unnamed kid, and John Grady Cole think beyond the comprehension of narrative, but they speak and act in full view. It is this occasional speech and resounding action that lend psychological texture to their respective identities. This is most certainly true of Billy Parham, who travels alone to hunt the spirit-wolf he quietly worships and in an act reminiscent of primordial ritual kills her to preserve her dignity.[24] He returns yet again to find his brother and, discovering that he is dead, in a gesture of grotesque heroism risks his own safety to take him home.[25] Throughout the novel he encounters the various outcasts who apprehend the spiritual yearning implied in his actions and speak to him as if he alone can understand. Billy emerges as a remarkable blend of character types: the young hero of the traditional bildungsroman, the mythic frontier American in the making, the outcast cowboy who lives in the vain hope that the land will survive. But he also reflects the orphan status of Ishmael in *Moby-Dick* and Alyosha in *The Brothers Karamazov,* since his external wanderings and crossings are mere projections of a tortured interior quest for the absolute, for a sense of purpose, an ordering principle that stands against the seeming chaos and indifference of the physical world. He thus becomes a character drawn from the romance tradition broadly construed, from the mythic

romances of Scott, Cooper, and Simms, and the psychological and metaphysical tradition of Hawthorne, Melville, Poe, and Dostoyevsky.

This generic framework exists primarily to allow for the exploration of philosophical issues, and it is the act of story-telling, the rearticulation of life in the form of narrative, that gives shape and meaning to these considerations. One of the most revealing passages comes from the priest who tells Billy the story of the pensioner, and in his speaking he moves straight to the point: "Who can dream of God. . . . Seated solely in the light of his own presence. Weaving the world. . . . A God with a fathomless capacity to bend all to an inscrutable purpose. Not chaos itself lay outside of that matrix. And somewhere in that tapestry that was the world in its making and in its unmaking was a thread that was he and he woke weeping" (149). Here the priest captures the sentiment that drives the pensioner back to Bavispe, where he will wrestle with the fates and with God himself after the tragic loss of his young son in an earthquake that devastated the town years before. McCarthy makes use of this aesthetic practice in various ways in different novels, but in *The Crossing,* he places extended monologues of multiple characters in parallel with one another in order to explore their sometimes tense interrelationships in a setting imbued in mystery. The image of the weaver-God is drawn from *Moby-Dick,* and like Melville, McCarthy writes with intense philosophical portent. But in *The Crossing* McCarthy is less ambiguous than Melville, since he posits an underlying unity in his characters' lives. In *The Crossing* the notion of individual stories unified in the "matrix" of the one story lends singularity to a multiplicity of perspectives. Early in the novel, the old man Billy encounters asserts the existence of a mysterious realm "invisible" to men, prefiguring the novel's

major trope of blindness, which has appeared before, especially in *Outer Dark*. In doing so, he provides a context for Billy's tortured quest for knowledge, which is externalized metaphorically in a journey during which Billy discovers meaning in the events he witnesses and receives insight into a divine order implied through the tales he hears from other witnesses. As Billy learns from the priest, these stories do not exist in isolation, for "rightly heard all tales are one" (143). The world woven into a complex tapestry by God is revealed by these various witnesses as involving one journey, one essential and universal drama of human strife and seeking.

It is here that McCarthy's reading in Georg Wilhelm Friedrich Hegel (1770–1831) becomes important, and given the centrality of Hegel to German Romanticism, a consideration of his thinking is helpful in coming to terms with the novel's philosophical themes.[26] In *Lectures on the History of Philosophy* (1805), *Encyclopedia* (1817), *Lectures on Aesthetics* (1818), *Philosophy of Fine Art* (1818), and *Lectures on the Philosophy of History* (1822), Hegel sees history as a record of the developing "World-Spirit," revealed through a "World-Process" and "Self-Realizing Idea." History involves a meaningful and divinely ordained forward movement, a poetic narrative in which humankind is the hero in a sweeping process of positive development. The refinement of human ideas, understanding, and linear time are co-implicated, since history involves a process in which provisional truths are posited as "thesis," counterbalanced in responses as "antithesis," then integrated in a "synthesis" of both, which forms the basis of a new and more developed "thesis." These notions are made concrete in the ideas that inform cultures, religions, intellectual paradigms, and institutions that are the material substance of history. In this way human conceptions

develop over time and are refined and perfected. History then is a grand "narrative," a kind of integrated and ordered story. For Hegel, the divine is present both inside and outside the process as the motivating force that lends direction, purpose, and meaning to history.

The priest Billy encounters at Huisiachepic, who in McCarthy's words "witnesses" to the tragic story of the pensioner, and the *gitano* he encounters toward the end of the novel, who tells him the story of the airplane, both argue for an essentially Hegelian account of the world and the human beings who occupy it, suggesting that individual lives, all of which have a narrative trajectory, converge in a kind of mystical synthesis in the matrix, the one tale, from which individuals find meaning in a given moment and in history broadly conceived. In the priest's tale, he tells Billy the sad story of the pensioner, how he loses his son in an earthquake and in a maddened state wanders the country seeking answers from God, finally passing the events to the priest who carries the tale forward, preserving it in memory. The priest recounts the story in the third person, and the central theme is the act of "witnessing," a term the priest uses a number of times. This witnessing is a form of telling that transcends mere reporting, and as the priest hears the pensioner's story the tale becomes his own and he wanders the country and speaks yet again to the events that have transformed him. It is through this act of empathetic rearticulation that human beings come to see how their individual lives are connected and their stories are one. In the priest's words, "It is God's grace alone that we are bound by this thread of life. Ultimately every man's path is every other's. There are no separate journeys. . . . All men are one and there is no other tale to tell" (156–57). Again, in the priest's words, told in the third person, "For the path of the world also

is one and there is no alter course in any least part of it for that course is fixed by God" (157–58).

In McCarthy's treatment the Hegelian notion of a history that achieves final culmination in an immediate encounter with the divine is never fully realize; nor is it challenged. Although characters in the novel live out the one story and their lives are presented in such a way as to emphasize the universal nature of the single journey, they never come to a complete and intellectually coherent understanding of the tale's purpose or meaning. Yet that meaning remains a distant reality built into the assumption that there is order in the one tale and implied purpose in its forward movement. The interchange between the priest and the pensioner, told to Billy, functions as one of the novel's thematic lynch-pins, making *The Crossing* itself an act of witness encompassing all the individual acts of its characters.

This concept of witnessing continues in the story of the blind man, who sits in relative silence as his wife recounts his experience to Billy. It is a horrific tale of revolution and violence in which the blind man's eyes are sucked from their sockets by a sadistic German commander in what at first appears as a kiss. The woman tells the story in great detail as if she were present, as if the experience is her own and her memory of it is perfect and immutable. McCarthy violates a basic principle in story-telling by allowing a second-hand account to render events in vivid clarity, but this violation is entirely consistent with his theme. Just as the husband's experience is the woman's as well, so it will become Billy's. Her retelling moves beyond the sensory, and her sense of its gravity and meaning allows her to delve beneath mere chronicle, since Wirtz, the German Huerista, is more than a single manifestation of brutish humanity and the blind man is more than a victim. The blind man as described in

the woman's imagination evokes the image of divine fire as seen in the epilogue of *Blood Meridian,* since "the red hole in his eyes glowed like lamps" (277). Conversely, Wirtz appears Satanic in proportions: "As if there were a deeper fire there that the demon had sucked forth" (277). She is absent from the events and the immediacy of the blind man's physical pain, but in her act of witness she comprehends a deeper significance in his suffering and eventual delivery, which reflect in small the existential condition of a human race fated to wander in blindness for a time but ultimately destined to be delivered from hunger and want to hearth and love, to the empathy present in the experience of the witness who in the retelling redeems the experience and ensures that it will never be lost. The woman speaks of the blind man's journey in a wilderness reminiscent of the Old and New Testaments, his attempted suicide, and his encounter with a mysterious man (reminiscent of a prophet or even a Christ figure) whose face at the blind man's touch seems ageless. As she concludes her story the blind man continues it, but before he does she establishes the thematic thread that will bind the two tales together and make them one. In her version, after his spiritual trial in an immensity of darkness, the blind man begins to see the world of appearances as unreal and illusory, and beneath that world resides an immaterial principle of order, since the world in darkness turns "with perfect cohesion in all its parts," in a realm beyond sensory apprehension. In the blind man's rendition, the moral status of the divine remains oddly impersonal, as human concepts of justice are blended with this abstract notion of order and purpose, where "in the deepest dark of loss . . . there was a ground" (292). The blind man's story ends ambiguously, since he tells of the just seeking after "righteousness," which in the end reveals itself simply as "order." But the ambiguity and

impersonal quality of this encounter with the numinous is enriched as it is understood, and that understanding is inseparable from the love of the woman and her intimate grasp of the truth of his experience, a truth and empathy they faithfully assume Billy will share as their mutual story becomes his own.

This re-creation of a single story through the act of witness is expressed again as Billy encounters the *gitano,* who has been hired to recover a plane in the mountains by the father of the dead pilot. Billy asks the *gitano* to clarify his purpose by telling the story of the plane. The man responds with three stories, denied later by an American who is traveling with them, but in doing so he explores the role of artifacts and the human apprehension of meaning in narrative. The father feels he must recover the plane so it will no longer have the power to "commandeer his dreams" (406). His desire suggests that there is a sacramental quality to physical artifacts as they reside in memory, and the *gitano* recovers two planes and is unconcerned which is the primary object of his quest. In playfully telling Billy the varied histories and concluding with a narrative account of a group of people seen in a set of old daguerreotype photographs, the *gitano* repudiates the notion that individual stories with distinctive meanings are contained in things, since "all past and all future and all stillborn dreams" are "cauterized in that brief encapture of light within the camera's closet" (412–13). Implicit in this consideration is Billy's own purpose in recovering Boyd's bones, which are themselves the artifacts of a presence that now resides only in memory. The grotesque quality of Billy's actions suggests the failure of objects to capture the essence of what is lost. On the one hand, the artifact itself remains a "husk," an empty receptacle of skeletal memory that falsifies the truth embodied in the story as it exists in actual history. The

movement of memory and the narrative inspired by artifacts recalls the boy's creation of the girl's life in "Wake for Susan" and John Wesley Rattner's fictive memory of his own past as he looks on at his mother's grave. In the end the objects evoke tales that may falsify the chronicle of history, and insofar as they are taken as history they become a form of "idolatry," a vain worship of lies. But when they inspire the act of telling, which continues in the perpetual act of witnessing, they initiate the narrative that through human seeking becomes the common experience of humanity. The literal truth defined in terms of historical veracity becomes secondary to the deeper truths that may be drawn from stories as they serve to define and enrich both the teller and the witness. Human lives then derive meaning and sustaining power as they participate in fictions that are more truthful than actualities bereft of purpose, since they are embodied with principles of unity, communal understanding, and intimations of the divine, principally as it is defined in terms of order, harmony, human intimacy, and finally in the only thing that can be seen as real—grace.

Still, some question remains as to the precise nature and the character of God, and McCarthy's adaptation of Melville's "weaver-god" is illuminating in this regard. In chapter 102 of *Moby-Dick,* "A Bower in the Arsacides," Ishmael describes the skeleton of "a great Sperm Whale" that has been carried inland by Solomon islanders and transformed into a temple and a trellis for the lush vegetation that surrounds it. For Ishmael, the earth is "a weaver's loom," the vegetation the "warp and woof," and the sunlight "a flying shuttle" operated by a silent, invisible, and ceaselessly working divinity that transcends the visible world. Yet this god paradoxically shares humanity's dilemma in this vast world-factory: "The weaver-god, he weaves; and by

that weaving is he deafened, that he hears no mortal voice; and by that humming, we, too, who look on the loom are deafened; and only when we escape it shall we hear the thousand voices that speak through it."[27] It is Melville's mysterious weaver-god, who is both inside and outside the eternal life-process, which the priest evokes and ponders. It is a conception that appears similar to the "panentheist" view that emerged in *Suttree,* in which the divine exists both within and outside his creation. As captured through the priest's tale of the pensioner, in eternally "weaving the world," this god, like Melville's, is in some way external to the "tapestry that was the world" and possessed of "a fathomless capacity to bend all to an inscrutable purpose." Yet he also seems bound within that world as a slave to "his own selfordinated duties" since "not chaos itself lay outside of that matrix" (149). This all-encompassing matrix thus functions like Melville's deafening "humming," which unites all the "voices" of humankind in a single inarticulate sound. The idea that one is merely a "thread" lost "somewhere in the tapestry that was the world in its making and in its unmaking" is not particularly consoling, for the priest wakes from his dream "weeping" as he considers the frightening implications of this possibility (149).

Yet there is perhaps an element of joy in the priest's tears, as he realizes that each of us takes an active role in weaving the matrix, in living and telling the individual tales that make up the one tale of the world. The priest's God resembles Hegel's World-Spirit operating through the creative activities of individual human beings.[28] But since this world of experience is often extremely brutal, *The Crossing* also relates to the questions of "theodicy," which is the effort among philosophers and theologians to reconcile God's benevolence with the omnipresence of evil in creation.[29] The God who presents himself in *The Crossing*

is one who offers fleeting glimpses of his presence but ultimately transcends human understanding. The fact of God's existence and tangible activity in the world is asserted by the priest, who articulates the pensioner's state of mind, "This man did not cease to believe in God. Nor did he come to have some modern view of God" (148). The priest's retelling of the pensioner's story and the belief system that emerges from it is not mere summary, since in the act of observing, listening, and witnessing, the "one" story has also become the priest's. The tales of the pensioner and the priest become the same narrative, as both alternately plead with God for answers and flee from him, not unlike Job and Jonah.

The dark epiphanies of both men are on the surface experienced by the actor (the pensioner) and articulated by the witness (the priest), but they are in fact experienced and told by both as one universal experience. The pensioner first narrates his epiphany to the priest, who witnesses this telling, and the priest then narrates the pensioner's tale to Billy and in so doing makes the pensioner's epiphany his own. Thus, the two epiphanies become different aspects of the same experience. The priest's words reflect a single revelation experienced by both the priest and the pensioner, expressing the same idea, and they coalesce in the notion of divine presence that has been present in McCarthy's work since *The Orchard Keeper* and is reflected in the mysterious sense of divine order clearly present in *Suttree, Blood Meridian, All the Pretty Horses,* and later in *No Country for Old Men* and *The Road.* As the priest asserts: "Deep in each man is the knowledge that something knows of his existence. . . . It was never that this man ceased to believe in God. No. It was rather that he came to believe terrible things of him" (148). He makes a claim with profound philosophical implications, arguing that

knowledge of a mysterious God whose actions are often inexplicable to man is not revealed in the logic or benevolence of those actions, but in a preexisting knowledge of the divine in human beings, an intuitive intimation of transcendence, which is revealed in language and finally in narrative. Thus, the human intellect and imagination are intimately involved with the activity of God, which is revealed in storytelling. In the priest's words, "In the end we shall all of us be only what we have made of God. For nothing is real save his grace" (158). By this logic, "grace" is associated with the power to narrate and resembles Hegel's World-Spirit working out its Self-Realizing Idea.

Still, the notion that revelation takes place in a narrative told and retold places the divine at some remove from the human perceiver, and there is much room for error and misperception. Thus, what we make of God, and by extension ourselves, may fall short of the ultimate reality of his grace, which is all that can be claimed as real, since grace is that which can be observed only in concrete terms in the human story, experienced by individuals such as the pensioner and witnessed through the empathetic retelling of the priest. These twin recognitions, the epiphany experienced by the priest and the pensioner, echo the central concerns of Job, insofar as they offer no satisfying answers to the problem of evil, nor do they seek to. They rest in the acknowledgment of the paradoxical action of grace—which reveals God's concern for humankind, demonstrated in the intimate connections Billy experiences with other human beings in his three crossings as well as in his devotion to his brother.

Even though every story takes its place in the one triumphant narrative that constitutes the history of the world, the climax and denouement of any individual journey may ultimately be tragic rather than epic, as the events of the novel often suggest. It is here we must note that McCarthy's use of Hegel in the novel

is by no means doctrinaire, insofar as the ultimate conclusion of the universal story is shrouded in the unknown. In both *The Crossing* and *Cities of the Plain*, after all, Billy's life is marred by failure and weakness. And yet a firm ethical foundation underlies his actions and relationships, and since the primary focus of the novel is the manner in which individuals derive meaning, this ethical foundation relates to the indirect revelation of God's grace in the grand narrative of human history. Ethics, then, lie in empathy and understanding, in identification with other human beings as each comes to grasp in an intimate way the common experience of all who comprise the human community. Billy's recovery of Boyd's bones in *The Crossing* and his dedication to John Grady Cole in *Cities of the Plain* suggest a moral compass and an ethos of self-sacrifice, and his actions imply his commitment to the road, a perhaps unconscious assent to the truth value implied in the tale itself and his purposeful role within it. This commitment to meaning and brotherhood is articulated to Billy early in *The Crossing* by an old Mexican:

> He told the boy that although he was huérfano still he must cease his wanderings and make for himself some place in the world because to wander in this way would become for him a passion and by this passion he would become estranged from men and so ultimately from himself. . . . He said that while the huérfano might feel that he no longer belonged among men he must set this feeling aside for he contained within him a largeness of spirit which men could see and that men would wish to know him and that the world would need him even as he needed the world for they were one. (134)

Huérfano translates as "orphan," which is significant in that Billy, the priest, and the pensioner, like Job and Melville's Ishmael, are

all metaphorically part of a single narrative of the lost child seeking origins and home. In one sense, Billy ignores the old man's advice, as he continues his wandering even into old age. But in *Cities of the Plain* he seeks that home in his relationship with John Grady Cole, choosing to define place not so much as physical locale but as the human brotherhood the old man values above wanderlust and the ill-conceived "passion" that would make him a kind of Melvillean isolato.[30] In this sense, the second two novels of the Border Trilogy continue the moral parable Edwin T. Arnold identifies in *All the Pretty Horses,* a parable that offers "an affirmation of life and of humanity, however severe the experience."[31]

Cities of the Plain (1998)

In the final novel in the Border Trilogy, McCarthy returns to his original conception: the simple story of two young men working a ranch near El Paso, passing their time in alternate realms of labor and reflection, as they witness the slow decline of range life and the birth of the nuclear age. The novel began as a screenplay written before the first two novels in the trilogy, and as such each work was likely written with the general outline of *Cities of the Plain* in mind. On first glance, the two main characters are quite similar, both mythic heroes of the old West who embody the values of simplicity and authenticity typical of the cowboy figure. But there are differences as well. In *Cities of the Plain,* John Grady Cole remains the consummate romantic, drawn to ideals of his own interior rendering as much as he is to the mystical reality embodied in the horses he nurtures and trains. Billy Parham is a character drawn more fully from the realist tradition, as his values center on friendship and principles of brotherhood and personal commitment. Given that both are protagonists in previous novels, this culminating story invites

an essential question: Who is the main character in *Cities of the Plain* and in the trilogy as a whole? The answer, though evasive, is deceptively simple: *Cities of the Plain* involves a single plot with at least two thematic emphases, each centering on a character. Which of them is most important depends upon which thematic strand one takes as central, which essential story draws the mind's eye. Insofar as *Cities of the Plain* is a serious western concerned with the confrontation of the old world and the new, of Mexico and America, and the destruction of the natural world by the cruel forces of modernity, John Grady Cole is the embodiment and tragic center of a firmly situated historical narrative. But for all its temporal grounding and resonance, the novel returns to one of McCarthy's basic concerns; that is, the tension between the ideal and the real, the interiors of human conception and the concrete fundamentals of the world, in essence, between dreams and their alternative in the tactile present.[32] These are issues central to John Grady Cole's character, but for all its focus on his heroic pursuits, the novel concludes with Billy Parham in old age contemplating these philosophical themes, and yet again McCarthy orchestrates Billy's silences precisely, and he becomes an important human figure through which essential questions are put in play. *Cities of the Plain* is at once a western full of romance and nostalgia strengthened by a sense of moral urgency inspired by the postwar years and the nuclear age. But it is equally a metaphysical and psychological romance preoccupied with the complexities of consciousness and the shaping forces of fate and human destiny. In this sense, John Grady and Billy are distinct and complimentary protagonists, whose concerns and motives animate a story of paradoxically profound simplicity.

Critical reception of the novel seemed to echo reviews of previous novels, although they contain few if any references to Faulkner. Reviewers in the major critical outlets seemed drawn

to the novel as a modern western and were somewhat taken by the sense of loss embodied both in character and landscape. In the *New York Times Book Review,* Sara Mosle begins by quoting Larry McMurtry: "One of the reasons the western has maintained its hold on our imagination . . . is because it offers an acceptable orientation to violence." With the exception of the final scene, the novel is not particularly violent, especially considering previous and even later works, but Mosle is compelled to remind readers of McCarthy's interest in brutality both in the human and natural sphere, writing that "his novels have descended on the dainty lawns of suburban fiction like a biblical plague."[33] It is the relationship of language to content that again seems the greatest critical preoccupation, and Mosle concedes that "The writing is often gorgeous" with "famously long sentences" that "suit his boundless terrain."[34] By placing the novel in the context of its historical setting, in the wake of two world wars and the global devastation that attended them, she argues that McCarthy's "grand style . . . gives the violence in his books a grandeur it doesn't deserve" claiming that "if we've learned nothing else about suffering in the twentieth century, it's that it's ordinary."[35] By implication this criticism applies to all McCarthy's works, which, regardless of setting, take the twentieth century as implicit context. But Mosle's assessment of the author's style is peculiar, since though *Cities of the Plain* is recognizably McCarthy, the word choice and sentence structure in the novel are vastly more direct and simple than elsewhere. In the *Chicago Tribune,* Alan Cheuse praises the novel in general, arguing that "if you love classic narrative, quest stories, adventure stories of high order transformed by one of the lapidary masters of contemporary American fiction, now is your hour of triumph." But he tempers his response by noting an aesthetic

departure, writing that "the style in this new work seems occasionally to bend . . . toward Hemingway's laconic stichomythia" with sentences that are more "declarative" than "revelatory."[36] Thus there is disagreement among critics regarding the role of representation, between artifice and the world portrayed, with Mosle preferring a simpler style but not finding it, and Cheuse recalling the "revelatory" quality of McCarthy's prose in previous works that perhaps animated his scenes with deeper levels of thematic texture. McCarthy's "late style," which might be characterized by a Hemingwayesque declarative simplicity, begins to emerge in *All the Pretty Horses*. In part, it disappears in *The Crossing* but begins to reappear in *Cities of the Plain,* and it achieves full expression in *No Country for Old Men* and *The Road.* But attempting to chart a linear stylistic trajectory is rife with difficulty. In spite of the common comparisons to Faulkner's work among critics, many of the southern novels contain passages characterized by a forceful minimalism, and for all its aesthetic density *The Crossing* often displays similar moments. In the *Concho River Review,* Jay Ellis notes a tendency toward implication in the first two novels of the Border Trilogy, writing that "this is characteristic of McCarthy. We have to look twice to see that he is careful not to tell all. . . . The consequences of the different crossings in the first two books are skillfully unwritten."[37] McCarthy shifts and blends the ornate and the declarative, the baroque and the laconic, and though individual novels may weigh in one aesthetic direction or the other, they tend to defy generalization. In the *Times Literary Supplement,* Paul Quinn observes this blending in the trilogy as a whole, writing that "the Border Trilogy . . . can be read, in part, as a movement between realms of language" in which "both types . . . can be seen as a response to the loss and absence

lining and defining the space between intension and expression."[38] For all the references to the western genre and to the violent content of previous works, with *Cities of the Plain* critics seemed particularly drawn to aesthetics, especially at the level of the sentence, and more broadly to the artifice of narrative forms that give substance and meaning to individual lives. In Alan Cheuse's terms, as he refers to the pictographs described in the novel, "The 'Border Trilogy,' now gracefully concluded, harks back to such ancient art, to the resonance of first stories, the kind we need to hear around the meetingfires."[39]

The title "Cities of the Plain" is drawn from chapter 19 of the book of Genesis, when—after establishing the covenant with Israel—Abraham attempts to stay God's hand against the iniquitous cities of Sodom and Gomorrah. But since the cities are bathed in sin, God enacts his justice: "Then the Lord rained on Sodom and Gomorrah" but "it came to pass, when God destroyed the cities of the plain, that God remembered Abraham, and sent Lot out of the midst of the overthrow, when he overthrew the cities in which Lot dwelt." The figure of God in this early biblical conception is active and multifaceted, concerned with human virtue and vice, willing both to destroy and redeem. In McCarthy's modern context, these cities of iniquity are El Paso, Texas; Alamogordo, New Mexico; and the border town of Ciudad Juárez, Mexico. It is autumn 1952, and John Grady Cole and Billy Parham are still committed to the range, as they work together on Mac McGovern's Cross Fours Ranch in Alamogordo. They exist in a congenial community of ranchers and cowboys, including Mac, his father-in-law Mr. Johnson, the cook and housekeeper Socorro, a fellow rancher Oren, and a collective of vaguely comic ranch hands such as Troy, Joaquin, and JC. Underlying this brotherhood is a pervasive sense of loss,

both for the way of life they struggle to maintain and for Mac's wife and Mr. Johnson's daughter Margaret, who died many years before and whom they remember with reverence and adoration. Billy is eight years older than John Grady. He is both a friend and a protector, and on their casual forays into the Juárez whorehouses John Grady falls in love with a beautiful but sickly prostitute Magdalena. The story's formal movement deftly negotiates between the depleted range and the town, between the harsh and indifferent landscape and the garish and sordid streets that make real the cities of the plain. Articulated as physical realms of rich symbolic import, these disparate settings are characterized respectively by the contrasting images of the horse and the taxicab, emblems of movement that typify the old and the new, the modern and the premodern. John Grady is still the mythic horseman, stubborn in his efforts to tame them yet possessed of a mystical ability to see into them and to communicate with the "justice" inherent in their "hearts." He is more than a practical man of work. He beats Mac at chess and understands enough of human avarice to thwart the dubious efforts of an unscrupulous horse dealer. Yet for all his physical skill, intuitive connection with nature, and intellectual savvy, he remains impractical and immovable in matters of love. He falls, under the most desperate of circumstances, for an ill-fated Mexican prostitute who is for all practical purposes the property of the pimp Eduardo, an otherworldly incarnation of evil as amoral as he is seemingly indomitable. She returns John Grady's love, and he elicits the aid of the reluctant Billy in recovering her from Juárez in order to marry her. But there seems to be a tragic dissonance between desire and realization, expressed fully in a conversation between Eduardo and Billy, and because in his own perverse manner he loves Magdalena as well, Eduardo would

rather see her dead than taken from him. He captures her in the act of escaping, and despite Billy's efforts the novel culminates in a knife fight that ends with Eduardo and John Grady fatally wounded. The action of the story has centered on John Grady, but Billy is always present, with some desperation seeking to alter the course of events. The novel concludes with an epilogue portraying Billy in old age, resting under an overpass in Arizona, his last job having been as a movie extra. He listens to the testimony of a mysterious, almost ghostly stranger, who tells a story of his dream of a "traveler" and his death by pagan sacrifice. The narrative thus blends the tactile realm of action, work, and daily living with the human interiors of desire, hope, and the ever-present reality of dreams, which as McCarthy renders them demand an equal claim upon the real. The surface of *Cities of the Plain* is substantial enough, dealing with the tensions and tragic implications of historical change and modernity in the twentieth century. But integrated with this story as observer and participant is Billy Parham both in his beginning and near his life's completion, silent but fully alive in interior consciousness and reflection, attempting to sort out the relationship between ideals and experience, and attracted always to the defining substance of dreams.

The novel's structure is quite simple, consisting of four untitled parts designated with Roman numerals that contain smaller sections separated at times with asterisks and at other times with section breaks between paragraphs, concluding with a lengthy epilogue. There is a largely contiguous narrative line that weaves its way through all the parts, as John Grady and Billy in the midst of their various conflicts move between the range and the sordid towns that draw them magnetically into the depravity of the modern world. McCarthy's liberal use of Spanish in

dialogue, more comprehensible in *All the Pretty Horses* and *The Crossing,* contains greater substance, and important content can be lost if one is unfamiliar with the language. What served a realist aesthetic in the first two novels in the trilogy is a bit of a problem in *Cities of the Plain,* as dialogue becomes a subtext requiring a Spanish language dictionary much like the author's archaic vocabulary often requires the *Oxford English Dictionary.* This obstacle is by no means insurmountable, and much can still be gleaned from context. The major interchanges between Billy and Eduardo, John Grady and Eduardo, and John Grady and the maestro are conducted in English. The dream that concludes the novel in the epilogue presents significant interpretive difficulties, but it also allows a certain freedom and opportunity for speculation, and the passage might be considered a key to the significance of character and events, much like the mysterious epilogue in *Blood Meridian.*

As a modern western, *Cities of the Plain* takes the cold war and the nuclear age as the stage upon which the drama unfolds. The story is set in part in Alamogordo, New Mexico. Mac acknowledges that the army will soon take over the ranch and that agents of federal government have been seen, that something ominous is occurring in the range country, which in the past was a place that offered freedom and simplicity even among the harsh conditions of the natural world. What readers recognize as the nuclear tests of the early 1950s appear as tangible historical events rich with symbolic implication, as the ubiquitous reach of the United States Government suggests more than itself, and seems a malevolent force of destruction that defies materiality and definition. The novel is distinctive in its promised focus on the "city," and in its own way reflects the urban setting in *Suttree,* which draws in part from the tradition of the American

city novel seen in the works of William Dean Howells, Frank Norris, Stephen Crane, Theodore Dreiser, Edith Wharton, Thomas Wolfe, Sinclair Lewis, and Upton Sinclair. The novel begins with a striking urban image: "They stood in the doorway and stomped the rain from their boots and swung their hats and wiped the water from their faces. Out in the street the rain slashed through the standing water driving the gaudy red and green colors of the neon signs to wander and seethe and rain danced on the steel tops of the cars parked along the curb" (3).

The young men soon enter a whorehouse, with disheveled prostitutes garbed in "shabby deshabille" sitting on "shabby sofas" in a barroom "all but empty." The bartender tells John Grady that he looks like a "wharf rat," and the entire scene recalls Knoxville's McAnally Flats as described in *Suttree*. Though these characters are somewhat less desperate, they form a similar community of the lost and fallen found in the earlier novel. The city is a degraded realm of waste and decay, and from the inception of the story sexuality and brutality are conjoined in a cruel yoking of potential opposites. The whorehouse and bar are the city's heart, and all that they imply of dissipation, exploitation, and decline is rendered fully, at times explicitly evoking the wasteland iconography of T. S. Eliot's poem: "They passed through the outskirts of the city . . . the river to the left through the river trees and the tall buildings of the city beyond that were in another country. . . . They passed the old abandoned municipal buildings. Rusted watertanks in a yard strewn with trash-papers the wind had left" (225). As perhaps is promised by the title, the city setting dominates the novel and is portrayed more evocatively than images of the natural world. Though vivid description of buildings, streets, barrooms, and watertanks abound, the city is animated by movement, and at the center is

the recurring image of the taxicab. The novel involves a series of alternating scenes in which John Grady and Billy traverse the range on horses and course their way through Ciudad Juárez in a hired automobile. Consistent with the historical themes of encroaching modernity, the landscape is a much-diminished thing, and while *All the Pretty Horses* and *The Crossing* are full of natural description, *Cities of the Plain* seems to suggest that even the open range in its farthest reaches cannot escape the machines of industry. In one striking scene, the natural and the artificial seem blended to a purpose: "In the mountains they saw deer in the headlights and in the headlights the deer were pale as ghosts and as soundless. They turned their eyes toward the unreckoned sun and sidled and grouped and leapt the bar ditch. . . . Troy held the whiskey up to the dashlights to check the level. . . . Be no lack of deer to hunt down here it looks like [Troy speaking]" (19). The image of a small group of wild deer is shrouded in a telling darkness and is illuminated only by an artificial light that transforms them into specter figures. The mountains in all their wildness are infused and perhaps corrupted in their purity by the boys in the car, and this image of the machine in the proverbial garden suggests the tension between nature and industry, the range and the city. While there are occasional descriptions of landscape in the novel, most involve this peculiar blending, and insofar as John Grady and Billy, even in their youth, represent the old order, their story is infused by a sense of loss that becomes more poignant since the meaning they derive from their experience on the range has much to do with the simple apprehension of beauty in the world, both in relationships and in the land itself. It is here that the cold war context becomes most informative, as the transformation of the natural to the artificial promises little in the way of hope and much in

the way of cataclysmic potential, perhaps in the form of nuclear war. Thus the pattern of conflict typical of the historical romance and the modern western, which pits the forces of progress and reaction against each other, becomes deeply portentous and tragic. This is made clear as John Grady encounters an old man on the road and they communicate without speaking, "As if they knew a secret between them, these two. Something of age and youth and their claims and the justice of those claims. . . . Above all a knowing deep in the bone that beauty and loss are one" (71). The historical narrative that centers on the destruction of the range by the forces of modernity becomes a compelling allegory of a universal human condition, in which the genuine apprehension and appreciation of beauty must occur in tandem with a sense of passing and the inherent transience of life, love, and perceived reality itself.

This transience defines the world of the real, the realm of tangible human perception. But McCarthy complicates this question as he deals with the contrast between the objective world of sense experience and the ideal world of dreams. At the center of this tension are John Grady, Billy, and Eduardo. As Billy enters White Lake to ask Eduardo to release Magdalena so that John Grady can marry her, Eduardo presents himself as the confirmed realist, and in dismissing John Grady's idealism as absurd, says that "men have in their minds a picture of how the world will be. . . . The world may be many different ways for them but there is one world that will never be and that is the world that they dream of. Do you believe that?" (134) Ishmael like, Billy's response is tentative, as he blandly acknowledges that perhaps he concurs without wanting to fully admit it. The force of Eduardo's expression lends some credibility to his assertions, but it is soon revealed that he is also in love with Magdalena and

as such is possessed of his own dream, willing to do all in his power, even through violence, to forge his own "mind's picture" from the raw substance of the world. Thus his professed realism is in part only feigned, and he emerges as John Grady's adversary not in a pitched battle between the ideal and the real, but in a conflict between two men, both driven by their love of a woman, who will sacrifice everything to transform hope into realization.

This forceful collision of conflicting dreams occurs in the final scene with John Grady and Eduardo. The pimp has had Magdalena murdered, and John Grady comes to White Lake to confront Eduardo and kill him in an act of righteous indignation and justified retribution. In his confidence and seeming indomitability, the pimp appears not unlike the judge in *Blood Meridian* and the Captain in *All the Pretty Horses*, as an incarnation of corruption and evil that is more than local but timeless. Unlike the judge, however, whose pronouncements abound with philosophical and religious overtones, Eduardo's musings are firmly human and political. Again, he deems John Grady's chivalry woefully naive. Before they begin their fight, Eduardo speaks, and continues to do so as they circle each other, slicing and lashing in a grotesque procession of incremental bloodletting. His most direct verbal attack at John Grady's idealism occurs as he places him in a class of young romantics, referring to them in general, saying, "They cannot seem to see that the most elementary fact concerning whores . . . is that they are whores" (249). This powerful claim highlights Eduardo's stark pragmatism, his bloody assent to the hard facts of human experience. There is an essential difference between him and John Grady insofar as he is Magdalena's pimp and he has continued up until her death to subjugate her as a prostitute. But again he was also in love with her, and as such he desires her at a deeper

level and in the end does not in actuality assent to the "fact" he espouses to John Grady. His masked idealism is certainly mitigated by the social conditions under which he lives, and this compromises his capacity for hope, his ability to conceptualize and dream as John Grady does. But he dreams nevertheless, and the imaginary realm he envisions, however poorly defined, has Magdalena before her death at its heart. His hardness at this moment might be seen as a response to her loss and the death of his ill-fated hopes. This disillusionment is forcefully expressed as their knife fight continues: "Your kind cannot bear that the world be ordinary. . . . But the Mexican world is a world of adornment only and underneath it is very plain indeed. While your world . . . totters on an unspoken labyrinth of questions. And we will devour you, my friend. You and all your pale empire" (253). This is a powerful proclamation that refers by implication to the adornments associated with Latin American Catholicism and the ornate artifice of Mexican art, culture, and ritual. They are metaphors for the capacity inherent in the human imagination to see beyond the everyday, sordid, and commonplace reality of human experience. In Eduardo's somewhat deceptive pronouncement, the ability to conceptualize realms of hope, possibility, and future potential, especially as they relate to love and human connection, are not only false but actively destructive, compromising the individual's and even the nation's ability to adapt to the hard realities of the natural world broadly conceived. Still it is important to consider this idea, not as a fully formulated worldview that defines Eduardo from the beginning, but as a powerful and even momentary epiphany born of loss and disillusionment. The fight continues as they parry with knives, and it is John Grady who watches Eduardo die, killing him by driving his mouth shut and stopping him from

speaking. In the end Billy Parham discovers his friend before his death, and he carries him through town taking him home. The pimp's bleak image of the world absent of dreams stands in contrast to the embodied friendship of the two young men and the powerful presence of Eduardo's own hope for a future with Magdalena. What remains is a tension even more unsettling than the surface pronouncements the pimp articulates. The world is not defined by a conflict between the ideal and the real, between human dreams and the indifference of physical law, but by a conflict of competing dreams and interior conceptions, dreams often precipitating acts of human violence that surpass any that may be found in the natural world. This appears in the epilogue, through the stranger's account to the seventy-eight-year-old Billy of the dream within a dream.

The epilogue begins with the young Billy leaving the ranch. Mac invites him to stay and tells him he will always have a job there, even when the army has taken the ranch, implying that his place will not be merely geographical but familial. It is Ash Wednesday, as is indicated by the fact that Socorro has been ritually marked by the cross indicating the mortality that defines them all. The scene swiftly shifts, with a surreal and dreamlike abruptness unmarked by line breaks or other transitional designators, and Billy is now seventy-eight years old in the second year of the new millennium. Having worked as a movie extra, he leaves the Gardner Hotel in El Paso and finds himself under a freeway overpass speaking with a strange man who for a moment he thinks may be Death itself. Though he denies it, the man is described in otherworldly terms and his physical features are such that Billy cannot determine his age. He is in this sense reminiscent of the mysterious wanderer in the wilderness who the blind man encounters in *The Crossing*, who at sightless

touch seems ageless. What follows is another of McCarthy's trademark interchanges between strangers who immediately connect in a distinctive form of spiritual intimacy, as the McCarthy protagonist, Alyosha like, listens in active silence to a narrative that becomes a compelling if mysterious rendering of his own experience half understood. After sharing a few crackers, Billy and the stranger begin discussing the portentous question of mortality. Billy asks, "Where do we go when we die?" and the stranger responds, "I don't know. . . . Where are we now?" (268). This question begins the man's tale of his dream in which he watches a "traveler" and sees within the traveler's own dream as he is taken captive in an ancient blood sacrifice. The narrative itself is rife with ambiguity and is difficult to comprehend fully, but at its heart it explores the blending of objective and subjective experience, reality and dream, considering the extent to which each can be called true and, as often appears in McCarthy's work, suggesting the limited scope of human understanding. Aware of the elliptical quality of the dream state, Billy asks the stranger if, though he perceived the traveler as separate, they were in fact the same person. The stranger responds that he doesn't know but that he doesn't think so, though none of us fully knows the substance of who we are, "But then if we do not know ourselves in the waking world what chance in dreams?" (271). The nature of the story that follows involves a paradoxical attempt to capture meaning while confronting the inherent limitations human beings face when sense perception in waking consciousness is their only point of reference. The stranger begins by speaking of a map he drew in middle age, when he was attempting to chart his own life's path and to grasp something of its ultimate direction. He drew the map in response to a dream, and it did little to predict his future. As he stresses

the substance and significance of sense perception, thought, interior reflection, and the unconscious, he claims that "every man is more than he supposes" (271), as each of these aspects of mind coalesce and blend: "But what is your life? Can you see it? It vanishes at its own appearance. . . . Until it vanishes to appear no more. When you look at the world is there a point in time when the seen becomes the remembered? How are they separate? It is that which is missing from our map and the picture that it makes" (273).

The map that charts the path of life is not without its truth value. But as a tactile figuration of the world it lacks explanatory power. Even as narrative or story involves the ordering of experience, possessing a universal quality (the main theme in *The Crossing*), so time is an illusion as human beings perceive it when they are fully conscious. When the dream-self is understood as a meaningful and important facet of human experience, the existing moment and memory are not as distinctive as they seem. Insofar as the map takes the passing of time as its defining element, it deceives even the cartographer himself. Time, lived experience, memory, conscious interior reflection, and dreams are blended in a woven tapestry and can never be fully distinguished or separated. Yet every map in its actuality is a reflection of every other, and there are meaning and substance in the world, the map, and the lives they chart, "For within their limitations there must be a common shape or shared domain between the telling and the told" (273). Here McCarthy returns to the role of the witness and the process by which the story of one life, through witness and retelling, becomes the story of all. In this sense, the traveler in the dream actually is the stranger, and in recounting the traveler's story his identity blends with Billy's as well, since in the stranger's words, "At the core of our life is the

history of which it is composed" and within it is "the act of knowing" that "we share in dreams and out" (281). Of course, there is a philosophical, religious, and moral dimension to the traveler's experience that speaks directly to McCarthy's preoccupation with violence. The traveler in the stranger's dream becomes the victim of a primitive ritual sacrifice, and his ordeal is simultaneously literal, metaphorical, and universal. The traveler's fate reflects the pattern of all human stories, and within it he becomes an "accomplice" in his own violent end. The dream scene harkens back to the ancient pictographs Billy and John Grady have previously seen, but the violence and bloodletting of these primitive peoples are no less horrific than the acts of the villainous Eduardo or the prospect of nuclear annihilation the novel takes as context. The traveler, like all human beings, becomes "accomplice in a blood ceremony that was then and is now an affront to God" (280). The universal story as articulated through the witness is rife with a violence that stands against the intentions and desires of the divine, and though this bloodletting is an essential part of the world, it exists in contrast to another aspect of experience that is equally compelling and real, in dreams as well as in waking consciousness.

The novel concludes as Billy, having found a home with a kind and selfless family near Portales, New Mexico, lives with them and sleeps in a shed near a kitchen that reminds him of his experiences as a boy. In a sense he has returned to childhood, as he calmly watches the children in the family when they come home from school and play with a young colt given to them as a gift by their father. In a way Billy becomes a member of the family, eating with them, playing cards, and telling stories of the range life of his youth. He still derives much meaning from the substance of interior reflection, and one night he dreams of

Boyd, who stands with him in the room but does not speak. It is a painful reminiscence as he recounts it to the woman of the house, who finds him afterward and offers to bring him a cup of water. She has heard him calling out Boyd's name, and Billy tells her the story in brief and confesses that his greatest desire is to see his brother. The woman speaks from her simple faith and tells him that his desire will in the end be granted. She looks at his hand and in a profound moment of empathy reads its lines and veins, seeing a map of universal significance, where there are "God's plenty of signs and wonders to make a landscape" (291). He wonders aloud at her willingness to take him in, confessing his own insignificance, but she sees something in him she never explains but feels drawn to sustain. To her, he is a man of the road wounded by a world that she understands. It is a world where the iniquities of human violence and depravity meet retribution—but in the end find a redemption that takes its life from acts of kindness and sympathy. Thus, even in its assent to the reality of violence and conflict inherent in the world, the trilogy concludes with an image of intimacy. Contained in this moment is hope, as well as faith in a genuine possibility: that the human community may in the end transcend time and material contingency. The map marks in definitive terms the iniquitous cities of the plain, where vice and malevolence define the patterns of experience, but infused and blended in its torn folds and vaguely discernable contours is a geography of peace and repose, seen in a moment when an old man torn asunder by loss finds solace in the simple words of a woman, who hears his plaintive call from sleep—and offers him water.

CHAPTER 5

The Later Works

While writing *All the Pretty Horses,* Cormac McCarthy began making regular trips from his home in El Paso to the Santa Fe Institute. In 1981 he was one of the first in the arts to receive the prestigious Genius Grant from the MacArthur Foundation. He attended a dinner in Chicago with other recipients and found himself spending time with scientists. Among them was the Nobel Prize–winning Murray Gell-Mann, a renowned particle physicist, the director of the MacArthur Foundation, and a longtime scholar at the Santa Fe Institute. Though they came from different backgrounds, the two men became good friends, and their association illuminates McCarthy's work at least from the Border Trilogy forward. Founded in 1984, the Santa Fe Institute is a think tank that brings together major intellectuals in a variety of disciplines, who conduct research in areas ranging from cell biology to chaos and complexity theory. The institute emerged when a group of scientists at the Los Alamos National Laboratory, home of the Manhattan Project after World War II, came together to establish a center where an array of intellectual fields might blend in interesting and productive ways. The leader was George Cowan, originally the head of research at Los Alamos, who served as president with Murray Gell-Mann as the chair of the board. This eclectic approach to a variety of questions was clearly attractive to McCarthy, who—after some years of limited association—moved to Santa Fe full time as a fellow. Though the author is firmly

rooted in the Euro-American literary tradition, in his later years he limited his reading in fiction and has spent much of his time exploring scientific issues. Although philosophical and scientific themes have been present in his works from the beginning, the western works display an overt concern with the material pattern of violence in the physical world. Though he has confessed a genuine admiration for scientific thinking, the works written between the final volume in the Border Trilogy and *The Road* tend to blend science with deep personal and theological concerns. These interests appear in his novels and dramatic work, particularly in "Whales and Men" (written in the mid to late 1980s), a dialogue-driven screenplay featuring a marine biologist, a wealthy explorer, and an Irish aristocrat who discuss whales and (reminiscent of *Moby-Dick*) define them in part as living symbols of impenetrable mystery.[1] Similar issues are at play later in *The Sunset Limited,* a "novel in dramatic form" published in 2006 and set in New York City.[2] After attempting to throw himself in front of a train, a college professor named White is rescued by an African American street preacher and former convict named Black. The play consists entirely of a debate, dealing primarily with human suffering and in that context the possibility, role, and nature of the divine. McCarthy is careful to balance the dialogue such that White's despair is answered effectively by the idiosyncratic hope of the preacher, who finds God's presence in daily human action grounded in selflessness. The play ends on an emotional counterpoint, as White's compelling words force Black into silence. In a plaintive prayer, Black admonishes God for not allowing him the verbal victory but commits himself in the end to a divine mission he only vaguely understands. *No Country for Old Men* and *The Road* involve these same issues, exploring again McCarthy's previous

concerns: the bleak reality of despair in world of violence, together with the human potential for self-sacrifice and intimacy.

No Country for Old Men (2005)

The Border Trilogy concluded, in *No Country for Old Men* Cormac McCarthy remains resolutely on the border, near a Texas town, among drug dealers and the dubious corporate interests that sustain them, amid working-class war veterans struggling daily for survival and the weak forces of law that attempt to stem the slow tide of violence that seems beyond containment. At the end of *Cities of the Plain,* which is set in 1952, the Mexican pimp Eduardo claims that "we will devour you, my friend. You and all your pale empire" (253). The "unspoken labyrinth of questions" Eduardo later refers to and the idealistic musings of a "pale" and "weak" American people might roughly characterize the thoughts of Sheriff Ed Tom Bell, who in an interlaced narrative strand laments the success of the avaricious world Eduardo predicted thirty years before. With its own particular alchemy, *No Country for Old Men* blends the popular American genre of the western and the crime novel, but it is a work of genre fiction nonetheless. In a western, it pits a lone Texas sheriff against a seemingly indomitable "black hat" who is as evasive as he is murderous. In a noir style crime narrative with clear cinematic potential, the sheriff seeks clues and follows their devious pathways through a bleak world of destructive potential he knows well by experience but only thinly comprehends.[3] The novel is a departure from anything McCarthy has written before, with a sentence-level style as spare and laconic as anything published in the contemporary period. In the *New York Times Book Review,* Walter Kirn ponders this shift in voice in the context of McCarthy's reputation, writing that "the late middle-aged

McCarthy found himself so thoroughly trussed in garlands and draped in medals that it's a wonder he could breathe." The author had been so commonly and favorably compared to his most-celebrated forebears in the American tradition that it is perhaps a wonder he didn't find it difficult to continue, since the pressure to out-write himself must have been tremendous. In Kirn's terms, since he was "designated as Hemingway and Faulkner's sole legitimate successor, he might have been wise to let his writing hand be removed at the wrist."[4] Of course, McCarthy's prose has often been associated with Faulkner's density of structure, expression, and word choice, and even in his earlier work, this comparison is more complicated and vexing than it may seem. Both authors share a willingness to employ the language experimentally, to carry syntax, subordination, and word choice in complex and interesting directions. But careful stylistic analysis reveals differences as well, particularly in Faulkner's tendency to employ multiple levels of subordination in stream of consciousness narrative, as compared to McCarthy's propensity to link independent clauses with the conjunction "and," thus creating extended lyrical passages with limited subordination. Kirn's reference to Hemingway is telling and comparatively rare in McCarthy criticism, and this latter stylistic practice is quite reminiscent of the earlier author. Although some may consider the simplicity in style that characterizes McCarthy's last two novels as a concession to the mass market, especially since both works were quickly adapted to film, it is perhaps more productive to observe this shift as yet another exploration of the potential of style and language broadly construed. In fact, *The Road* contains explicit allusions to Hemingway, and the sentence structure in both late novels reflects more fully the minimalist aesthetic that Hemingway in

part founded, an artistic practice common in modern and contemporary prose fiction, particularly in the short-story form. Thus McCarthy's late style is influenced by another strand in the complex and varied literary tradition that immediately precedes him, and his subject matter remains bleak and unremittingly harsh, for the most part unappealing to a general audience.

The departure in *No Country for Old Men* displays a preoccupation with style itself, in all its variety and diversity, as well as with the fluid possibilities of popular literary genre. Although the story has a pulp quality, in its intensity and latent philosophical preoccupations it remains unbound by formal rules. Still, as Kirn notes, it is "a darting movie-ready narrative that rips along like hell on wheels because it has no desire to break new ground, only to burn rubber on hard-packed old ground, thereby packing it down harder."[5] Kirn's rhetorical flourish illuminates the role of genre in the novel, since both the western and the crime novel take violence as their primary subject but deal with them with varying levels of intensity. In *No Country for Old Men,* McCarthy twists these pulp genres, and in doing so frustrates readers of popular novels who come to the narrative with fixed expectations as to the nature of character and the outcome of plot. In a blurb for a paperback edition, Sam Shepard observes these complexities, characterizing the novel as "a monster of a book" in which McCarthy achieves "monumental results by a kind of drip-by-drip process of ruthless simplicity" leaving the reader "panting and awestruck." The novel began as a screenplay, which makes sense considering that Sheriff Bell's interior monologues are written such that they might be easily excised in voice over, and the main narrative is simple, vivid, and weighted heavily in the direction of dialogue. Though it is McCarthy's first work after the Border Trilogy, it is the fifth set in the West, and

it involves a further exploration of the nature and reach of human violence, as well as the capacity of individuals to control the changing circumstances that contain and propel them. The film rights to *No Country for Old Men* were quickly optioned by Paramount and the film was released in 2007. Written and directed by Joel and Ethan Coen, it garnered international acclaim, winning four Academy Awards including Best Picture, as well as major awards from the National Board of Review, the Directors Guild of America, the New York Film Critics Circle, and the Golden Palm at the Cannes Film Festival, among others.[6]

The novel is set in 1982 in and around the small south Texas town of Sanderson, near the Mexico border. Sheriff Ed Tom Bell, a World War II veteran and a descendent of a long line of Texas lawmen, struggles to maintain the peace amid the escalating violence of the drug trade. In his early career, he met little conflict, sending only one criminal to death row. But the malevolence he has encountered is perplexing to him, and he struggles to understand the motives that drive people to acts of brutality and at least initially concludes that the world is getting worse, that his efforts are ineffective in responding to the harsh realities of human avarice in the late twentieth century. Though critical of himself, he takes solace in his marriage, crediting his wife with grounding him and giving his life a sense of meaning and value, saying that "marryin her makes up for ever dumb thing I ever done" (133). The main narrative begins as a local welder and Vietnam veteran, Llewellyn Moss, while hunting antelope near the Rio Grande, finds the vehicles and bodies of a group of drug runners who have killed one another in an exchange gone wrong. In a moment of temptation and weakness, Moss unwisely leaves with a satchel containing two million dollars. The satchel hides a radio transponder, and he finds himself fleeing

from a number of people who seek the money—most important, the single-minded psychopath Anton Chigurh, who murders without remorse in accord with an inexplicable set of principles grounded in a vaguely articulated deterministic philosophy. Chigurh contends that his free choice to kill is mitigated by an elaborate system of cause and effect that renders individual agency largely inconsequential. Moss sends his young wife, Carla Jean, to her grandmother's home in Odessa, and the novel involves the process by which Chigurh seeks Moss, and Ed Tom Bell desperately tries to stem the violent outcome and return Moss to his wife. In the end, however, Moss and Carla Jean are killed, Chigurh (a kind of "ghost") finally disappears, and Bell, having retired, is left to contemplate the nature of violence, his own purpose and value, and the moral and religious implications of the life he has lived and the world he has seen.

For all its assent to the popular, the novel takes its title from William Butler Yeats's "Sailing to Byzantium," among the most widely anthologized poems of twentieth-century literature. The lyric begins "That is no country for old men," referring to an artless world of impermanence and sensual pleasure, which contrasts with the timeless world of beauty, evident in great works of art, specifically those of the post-Roman Byzantine Empire. The reference is clearly to Ed Tom Bell, his uncle Ellis (a former sheriff who enters briefly late in the story), as well as the harsh world of violence and struggle they work to control and understand. The novel presents fewer intellectual challenges since its style is direct, with virtually no archaic vocabulary and few syntactic complexities. The sentences are reminiscent of Hemingway's, as are the characters, and Hemingway's influence on the novel is reinforced by McCarthy's deliberate allusions to his predecessor's works in *The Road*. The narrative involves two

interlaced strands that are clearly distinguishable, the first being Ed Tom Bell's extended interior monologue, printed in italics, and the second the main storyline, which involves Llewellyn Moss, Carla Jean Moss, Anton Chigurh, and Ed Tom Bell. The monologue takes the story as subtext but does not substantially refer to events that occur in the primary narrative, and the sheriff's reflections shift between intense inquiries into the nature and reach of violence and more casual but nonetheless touching comments about his wife and the sustaining value of their marriage. The main narrative is driven by scenes and dialogue and as such is quickly paced. Both strands encourage a blend of objective and subjective modes of perception, as the tangible events in the material world stand together with a detailed, plaintive, and occasionally heart-rending consideration of its meaning.

As he attempts to sort out the events he has witnessed and the life he has lived, Ed Tom Bell feels overmatched, unable to contend with forms of violence that seem monstrous in proportion to those other sheriffs have dealt with in the past. He loves to hear stories of the old-time lawmen—the ethical standards that defined their behavior, the stoic resolve with which they confronted a harsh world. But initially he contends that their circumstances were less formidable, as he recalls one ancestor who worked as a sheriff but didn't even carry a gun. He imagines a past defined by virtue and social order, an ethos of personal responsibility reflected in manners and pristine codes of external behavior. As he ponders the decay of that world, he is concerned not so much about personal safety but about the outcome of his overexposure to evil: "*I cant say that it's even what you are willin to do. . . . I think it is more like what you are willin to become. And I think a man would have to put his soul at*

hazard. And I won't do that. I think now that maybe I never would" (4). The world is rife with a violence that he is drawn to contemplate and understand, as he reads the papers and ponders incidents of murder and psychopathology. In doing this he reflects upon the wisdom of his wife, Loretta, who has made a deliberate decision to limit her exposure. Even as he performs his duties and explores these questions, he acknowledges her wisdom, saying, *"My wife wont read the papers no more. She's probably right. She generally is"* (40). But the extraordinary nature of the modern moment compels him, as he remembers the one young man he sent to execution, who murdered without motive, purpose, logic, or regret. This becomes clear in a chilling confession as Bell recounts it: *"I sent one boy to the gaschamber at Huntsville. . . . My arrest and my testimony . . . He'd killed a fourteen year old girl. . . . And he told me that he had been plannin to kill somebody for about as long as he could remember. Said that if they turned him out he'd do it again"* (1). The boy's malevolence is chilling and is configured more fully in Anton Chigurh as the novel proceeds. But Ed Tom Bell is unable to separate his direct experience of evil from his memories of the past, and his reflections are notably reactionary, since he thinks the brutality of the modern moment is more forceful and prevalent than in previous generations. The boy's lack of motive and the sense of mystery that surrounds him suggest a form of evil that transcends time and place, and in experiencing its stunning frankness as the boy expresses it, Bell misapprehends its nature, associating it with a twentieth-century environment characterized by the drug trade. Later Chigurh's actions serve to further define in words the brutality the boy thinly exemplifies, and in the philosophical musings that often precede his murders, Chigurh becomes an omnipresent force of evil that is metaphysical by

implication. Even in Bell's initial misapprehension, he begins to intimate this, saying that "*somewhere out there is a true and living prophet of destruction and I don't want to confront him. I know he's real. I have seen his work*" (2). Though he has not come to a full recognition of the historical breadth of this ubiquitous evil, his monologue begins to reflect more clearly McCarthy's own assessment of human brutality in the Woodward interview, when he claims, "There's no such thing as life without bloodshed. . . . I think the notion that the species can be improved in some way . . . is a really dangerous idea."[7] Bell's initial view of his current situation stands in contrast to the notion that the world has always been defined in part by bloody competition and violence, but it captures a sense of moral urgency and a desire for peace not apparent in McCarthy in the interview. Though it is inappropriate to conflate McCarthy with one of his characters, it seems reasonable to assume that, for all his fatalism, the author by no means accepts the bloodshed he often portrays. The monologue deals with the intricacies and personal tensions of a man attempting to understand the power of violence in a changing world, and it does so in a deliberate homage to the hard-boiled novels of the noir genre, particularly in the hands of Dashiell Hammett, Raymond Chandler, Jonathan Latimer, and Erle Stanley Gardner, in which the detective ponders in first-person narrative the darkening world that confines him and dictates the ethical terms of his actions.

Though Llewellyn Moss is an important character in the main narrative, a protagonist in the sense that readers are encouraged to sympathize with his plight, the story centers on the character of Anton Chigurh. The peculiar, measured, and philosophically portentous logic that attends his actions is rich with implications, insofar as it sheds light on the questions Ed

Tom Bell struggles to answer. Throughout the novel, McCarthy lends this villain's character a mythic and otherworldly quality, not unlike his many other avatars of evil—the triune in *Outer Dark,* Judge Holden in *Blood Meridian,* even Eduardo in *Cities of the Plain.* From the onset, to the reader familiar with Mc-Carthy it seems unlikely he will ever be captured or his malevolence contained. Carson Wells, the former lieutenant colonel who is hired to kill him, describes him as a "psychopath," and this term is by no means inappropriate. But he is also "sociopathic" insofar as he lives a life unencumbered by social obligation or responsibility to any preconceived moral precepts. His worldview is well considered and philosophically constituted, which becomes clear when he finds Carson Wells. With his shotgun calmly poised to kill him, Chigurh says, "You should admit your situation," and Wells responds, "Do you have any notion of how goddamned crazy you are?" (175). Chigurh's chilling answer: "The nature of this conversation?" (175). The killer's presumed insanity is the natural outcome of a deterministic philosophy prefigured in the dialogue between John Grady Cole and Dueña Alfonsa in *All the Pretty Horses,* when they ponder the role of fate, chance, and choice through the metaphor of the coin toss. The same chaos theory that formed the intellectual basis for that conversation motivates the thoughts and actions of Anton Chigurh.

It is essential to begin any inquiry into Chigurh's character by piecing together elements of his perspective on the God question. Late in the novel as he is about to offer the coin toss to Carla Jean Moss, he alludes to his lack of religiosity indirectly, saying, "Even a nonbeliever might find it useful to model himself after God. Very useful, in fact" (256). The God he imagines is by no means a deity of benevolence and concern but is instead an

abstract and indifferent lawgiver concerned with balancing the cosmic scales in the interest of principles beyond human understanding. The essential point, however, is that Chigurh characterizes himself as a nonbeliever, and the fact that he models himself upon God is perhaps best taken as a playful attack on the deity his victim takes as real. As with the garage attendant earlier in the novel, he offers Carla Jean an opportunity for salvation. He asks her to call the toss in the hope of saving her life. In *All the Pretty Horses,* the coiner casts the alternate sides of the coin and sets the course of human fate in motion. The coin now rests in Chigurh's hands. From his point of view, consistent with chaos theory, an irreducibly complex matrix of cause and effect has brought them both to the present moment, and though chance governs the fall of the coin, it is a chance mitigated by all the intricate consequential moments that precede it. Even the portentous fortune in the toss is circumscribed by time and previous events, and the fact that Chigurh could act out of free will, choosing not to kill, is from his point of view a comforting illusion devoid of truth. Though he freely told Llewellyn his life was forfeit, he offered him the opportunity to save Carla Jean by returning the money. Not trusting him, Moss refused to do so. That decision was one of many events that led to the here and now, and in the strange logic of Chigurh's determinism, he presents the coin toss as the one chance to chart the sequence differently and preserve her life. From his perspective, he is merely an actor in a rigidly determined historical process. She initially refuses to call the coin, claiming that God himself would not sanction the act, but Chigurh responds that the God she believes in would certainly want her to try. In the end, she assents and loses, and before he takes her life Chigurh interprets the circumstances that have led them both to this precipitous moment: "I

had no say in the matter. Every moment in your life is a turning and every one a choosing. Somewhere you made a choice. The accounting is scrupulous. The shape is drawn. No line can be erased. I had no belief in your ability to move a coin to your bidding. How could you? A person's path through the world seldom changes and even more seldom will it change abruptly" (259).

Chigurh begins by defining his role in the events that will lead to her murder. He acknowledges the reality of volition, but the choice was Carla Jean's as well. Though her decision to marry Llewellyn Moss seemed inconsequential at the time, the outcome of that choice is cataclysmic in its consequences and entirely unpredictable. It is again the central metaphor of chaos theory— the butterfly flapping its wings in New York causing a typhoon in the South Seas.[8] Every volitional act is ironically both meaningful and meaningless, meaningful insofar as it is an essential part of an ultimate destiny, meaningless since its consequences cannot be controlled. The course of history and human lives proceed independent of free will, and prediction is impossible in the closed and highly complex physical system that is the world. Certainly, Chigurh might "choose" not to kill Carla Jean. He might "choose" a life of benevolence and decency. But from his point of view the world would not change as a result: its violence and indifference to human life are pervasive, and the cause and effect that constitute the universe are entirely determined and rife with suffering and bloodshed.

Like the pronouncements of Judge Holden and Eduardo, Chigurh's thinking is bound within his character and should be taken as only one thread in the thematic texture of the novel. His logic, particularly in its antireligious implications, stands in contrast to the motives, hopes, and dreams of Ed Tom Bell. In spite

of Bell's desperation, he continually reflects upon his fortune, especially his marriage to Loretta, and he associates this luck with divine providence, saying, "*I don't recall that I ever give the good Lord all that much cause to smile on me. But he did*" (91). This rather conventional assent to God is complicated toward the end of the novel by his lengthy conversation with Uncle Ellis as well as his portentous dream of his father. After deciding to retire, he visits Ellis at his dilapidated home. The old man is confined to a wheelchair as a result of a gunshot he took in the line of duty as a sheriff. There is an endearing, even-comic quality to the scene, as Ellis offers Bell a cup of week-old coffee and is surrounded by cats he describes as "outlaws." The old man is curious about Ed Tom's decision to leave his job, and this leads to a discussion of violence and the role of God in a world pervasively shaped by destruction. Bell confesses that the medals he received in the war were undeserved, but Ellis contradicts him, and as they ponder the brutality they have seen, Ellis accepts the existence of God but questions His ability to control the universe He has presumably set in motion. From Ellis's point of view, Ed Tom Bell is wrong in considering the world more cruel now than in the past. Evil is an ever-present reality standing in perpetual conflict with the decency that may be found in human relationships. This insight conditions the content of Bell's evocative dream at the end of the novel, in which he sees his father carrying a gourd of fire into a pervasive darkness. In the dream he ponders the meaning of the fire, and this final segment in Ed Tom's reflection functions much like the epilogues in *Blood Meridian* and *Cities of the Plain*. In the epilogue of the former novel, a mysterious man strikes holes in the floor of the desert, releasing a fire that suggests the principle of divine order that underlies all that can be seen as real. The fire in Bell's dream takes on a more personal

quality, and meaning is associated with human intimacy even in darkness: "*And in the dream I knew that he* [his father] *was goin on ahead and that he was fixin to make a fire out there in all that dark and all that cold and I knew that whenever I got there he would be there*" (309). It is a dream, and in McCarthy's world of ambiguous shadow its credibility is suspect. The fire suggests warmth, hope, survival, illumination in the darkness of cosmological oblivion, and—given his discussion with Uncle Ellis—the divine. While it may merely reflect Bell's desperate hope amid the hard reality of the world, it emerges from his memory of fatherhood and it tallies with his deeply fulfilling experience of marriage. The novel then, for all its evocation of malevolence and brutish reality, concludes on an intimation of possibility and light, linked vaguely to the divine, perhaps, but firmly to the redemptive power that grows from the bonds of human community.

The Road (2006)

Barely a year after *No Country for Old Men,* Cormac McCarthy released perhaps his most searing, emotionally intense, and deeply personal novel. It is the story of a nameless father and son traveling through a postapocalyptic landscape in a hopeless attempt to survive. The novel quickly emerges as a parable, a kind of biblical allegory that blends figurative and mythic qualities with the intimate emotional textures that naturally bind a parent and a child. In many ways a departure from earlier works, *The Road* maintains McCarthy's consistent focus on the extremes of human experience, in this case in a wholly imagined realm of global annihilation. It is a setting that previous novels, often in the extended, nightmarish, even prophetic words of various characters, have anticipated and encouraged readers to fear. In his one television interview, McCarthy described the genesis

of *The Road*. Late at night he stood in a hotel room in El Paso, his young son John quietly sleeping in the bed near him. He looked out of the window and imagined the world in fifty or a hundred years, void of light and life, devastated beyond recognition. When asked what he wanted readers to take away from the novel, his response was precise yet paradoxical: "That we should be grateful." The image of his young son peacefully resting in a world still living suggests an almost sentimental hope, even an admonition that collectively we stem the tides of human devastation, whether nuclear, environmental, or social. But tension emerges when the novel is read with the memory of Judge Holden's fatalistic and celebratory claims about the divinity of war, or Eduardo's (perhaps feigned) description of the "plain" reality of a wasted world, where all beauty is mere "adornment." In this context, the imaginary world of *The Road* seems the blighted end of a natural evolutionary process, informed perhaps by a mysterious and morally ambiguous metaphysics, with horror and bloodletting at its heart's core. Unlike some of McCarthy's previous novels, however, the center of this road narrative is character relations, the touching and embodied relationship of father and son. Their interchanges are terse but frequent, and much in the way of emotional intensity is effectively implied, often reinforced by brief moments of interior reflection from the point of view of the man. While this relationship is grounded in the world of action, practical thought, and survival, it takes its life from a mystery that transcends material contingency and instinct, as their bond is consistently linked with the divine, with "God," however inadequately understood. In the same interview, McCarthy seemed to invite the God question, which came after his comment about gratitude. Oprah Winfrey asked: "So you haven't got the whole God thing worked out?"

Underneath what might have seemed an evasive answer, his response was direct: "It would depend on what day you asked me. . . . Sometimes it's good to pray. I don't think you have to have a clear idea of who or what God is to pray. You could even be quite doubtful about the whole business." To read the novel too narrowly in the context of these comments is inappropriate given the mysterious process by which thought and perspective find expression in literary art. However, McCarthy's words are illuminating, especially considering the moment with his son when the novel was conceived, insofar as they reveal one essential truth: the question of the divine in his conception is blended with and highly pertinent to any consideration of human intimacy. In this sense the novel is a narrative of the soul's nature: its moral embodiment in human form; its visibility in human action, whether in acts of brutality or self-sacrifice. *The Road* also explores the soul's capacity to transcend, perhaps in passing moments of hope, and more important in the permanent inscription of the Word, gone now from the pages of books, but resident with latent emotional force in human memory.

Surpassing even *All the Pretty Horses* in popularity, and at least rivaling *Blood Meridian* and *The Crossing* in its varied but often enthusiastic critical reception, the novel was widely reviewed and vigorously promoted, eventually winning the Pulitzer Prize. It was immediately optioned for cinema adaptation by 2929 Productions, Metro-Goldwyn-Mayer, and Dimension Films. Produced under the direction of John Hillcoat, the film was released internationally in the spring of 2009. Critics of the novel were quick to note the minimalist aesthetic driving the language—in description, interior reflection, and dialogue. In the *New York Times,* Janet Maslin writes: "This parable is . . . trenchant and terrifying, written with stripped-down urgency

and fueled by the force of a universal nightmare." For Maslin, though the visual intensity of a wasted world foregrounds his "pessimism," marked by "a dark fascination with the primal laws of survival," it is a story "more radiant than it is punishing."[9] In the *New York Times Book Review*, the novelist William Kennedy echoes these sentiments, especially with regard to style, arguing that "*The Road* is the most readable of his works, and consistently brilliant in its imagining of the posthumous condition of nature and civilization."[10] Kennedy is rather single-minded as he considers McCarthy's themes in general, which in his view involve the unambiguous triumph of evil. This is an extreme assessment given that in McCarthy's previous works goodness often resonates, alive however tenuous, embodied in friendships as well as in moments of self-sacrifice and stoic resistance. Still, Kennedy sees a redemptive potential more fully expressed in *The Road*, claiming that "evil victorious is not this book's theme" since "McCarthy changes the odds to favor the man and boy."[11] Referring to the often-passionate debate that centers on McCarthy's style, however, Kennedy prefers the more baroque and overtly poetic language of earlier novels. In his view, the language in previous works contains a more dense and compelling psychological texture, and he concludes that *The Road* is "brief and mystical" but perhaps too "austere," limited by a "scarcity of thought in the novel's mystical infrastructure" which "leaves the boy a designated but unsubstantiated messiah."[12] Reviewers of the novel frequently point to the biblical allusions and resonances, reading it as a "parable" and a "pilgrimage" of profound spiritual implications. In the *London Review of Books*, Philip Connors claims: "He has spent forty years writing as if he were trying to expand the Old Testament. With this latest novel he appears to want to build a bridge to the

New."[13] Like Kennedy, Connors notes the messianic quality rather unambiguously presented in the boy's character, which implies not only the moral purity and self-sacrifice of Christ, but also the political and religious strife that led to his execution, since the decimated world of *The Road* may have emerged from a war in which social and sectarian motives were involved. Connors makes direct reference to the religious and philosophical themes, noting that the story deals directly with the role of God in human affairs, the possibility of an active and benevolent deity, as well as McCarthy's measured ambiguity on these matters. Connors writes, "The curious thing about the novel is McCarthy's refusal to referee this argument."[14] What is clear in these initial critical assessments is that *The Road* attempts to blend ideas common in religious parables with the more detailed intensities of the human bond, as well as with the force of human will in the context of love and reverence. Unlike previous McCarthy novels, which must be read slowly to be appreciated, *The Road* is imbued with a sense of urgency, as if essential truths that cannot be spoken clearly must nevertheless find imperfect expression in language, in the broken words that form the human analog of creation, the "vermiculate patterns" that are "maps of the world in its becoming" (287).

The novel begins roughly ten years after a catastrophe has left the world thinly populated by the wandering remnants of humanity, who instinctively seek food in a primal quest to survive. They are often driven by impulses opposed to reason, since to a rational intellect death might be preferable. A man and his young son travel a nameless road that from the topography appears to course through a pass in the southeastern United States. They are heading toward the coast. The nature of the catastrophe is unclear, and the description of the blighted

landscape suggests nuclear winter, or, conversely, the effects of a large meteorite or the collision of an asteroid. It is certain, though, that the disaster occurred in an instant: "The clocks stopped at 1:17. A long shear of light and then a series of low concussions" (52). The language as articulated seems selected for its ambiguity, allowing for both possibilities, which have vastly different implications. A nuclear holocaust would be the result of human evil, and the meteor or asteroid the outcome of natural evil and the destructive capacity of the universe broadly construed. This blending suggests perhaps that the two are co-implicated and inseparable. The time is precisely stated with an emblematic intensity, and though the symbolic meaning of the numbers cannot be determined with any certainty, it evokes Revelation 1:17 and the dream vision of John the Divine, in which he witnesses the Second Coming of Christ. In verses 16–17, John recalls: "And he had in his right hand seven stars: and out of his mouth went a sharp two-edged sword: and his countenance *was* as the sun shineth in his strength. And when I saw him, I fell at his feet as dead. And he laid his right hand upon me, saying unto me, Fear not; I am the first and the last." Christ's face is compared to the sharp "light" of the sun, implicitly "shearing" in its association with the "two-edged sword," holding stars that will appear throughout the novel as the man and the boy continually look past the gray and wasted world into the night sky. It is an image of power and destruction as well as hope and light, and it speaks both comfort and commandment, with Christ demanding that his presence be recorded in words, the allusion suggesting that the novel as parable is a kind of prophesy. In verse 19, Christ continues: "Write the things which thou hast seen, and the things which are, and the things which shall be hereafter." The boy was not yet born when the event hit, and the two of

them travel alone, abandoned by the wife and mother who killed herself with a shard of obsidian after a period of hopeless and tortured reflection. The father struggles with these same thoughts, but he is utterly committed to the boy as they push a shopping cart in search of food, blankets, anything that will enhance their chances to survive another day. On the road, they meet strangers in desperation, corpses and skulls, and other grotesque remnants of waste and destruction, as they seek to avoid the roving clans of "bad guys" who have long ago abandoned civil rule and survive on the flesh of other human beings. The touching love and commitment of father and son is ironically enriched by the conflict that emerges between them, as the man fights the same hopeless despair that led his wife to suicide, yet finds himself willing to violate moral principle to ensure their survival. With the inarticulate but strangely mature insight of a child, the boy demands that they remain "good guys," a status they can rightfully claim only if they give food to the hapless outcasts they occasionally meet. The father is sympathetic but conflicted, and after killing a man who threatens them, he tells the boy: "My job is to take care of you. I was appointed to do that by God. I will kill anyone who touches you. Do you understand?" (77). It is an ambiguous comfort for the boy, who is more than a starving child but a messianic figure in a lost world, in the father's own words a "Golden chalice, good to house a god" (75). The boy takes solace in the father's strength but is disheartened by his willingness to defy ethics in the interest of survival. In his young mind, what matters most is the "goodness" he has only seen in dreams, in the stories his father has told him, which recall incidents and images of the world before the apocalypse. As they travel, an ominous and bleak truth attends them: the father is coughing blood, and readers are given to understand

that eventually he will die, leaving the boy alone in a land bereft of hope. In spite of this, throughout their journey they are strangely attended by "luck," narrowly escaping threats and finding the food and other necessities that sustain them. The novel, then, recounts a struggle for more than survival. It is a contest of instinct and ethics, body and spirit, hope and despair.

As William Kennedy claims in the *New York Times Book Review,* the story—especially when compared to many of McCarthy's earlier novels—is quickly paced and readable. Essentially a journey narrative, it draws from the popular genre of the apocalyptic novel, the postapocalyptic and dystopian narrative, as well as from the wasteland iconography of medieval legend and T. S. Eliot's poem. Descriptions of setting evoke the wilderness typology of the Old and New Testaments. In its treatment of corpses, cannibalism, the extremes of human avarice, and ubiquitous decay, the novel features elements of the gothic, and though set in an unnamed southern locale, this genre motif is by no means specific to region. Instead, much like *Outer Dark,* it has a mythic quality and is broadly descriptive of a universal human condition. There are no chapter breaks, but the narrative line is direct, and events as well as thoughts are divided by line separations between paragraphs and occasional ellipses that mark more distinctive pauses. At times, there is a dreamlike quality apparent even in narrative structure, as dialogue, physical description, as well as personal reflection, are blended in a strange pastiche of expressive modes. While most of the story involves a combination of third-person limited omniscient narrative and conversation, there are occasional and often brief vignettes of intense interior monologue on the part of the father. The overall style is minimalist and reminiscent of Ernest Hemingway, and McCarthy orchestrates an homage to his predecessor in a

number of vivid allusions. As the third-person narrator recounts the father's memory of the boy's birth, the mother's pain and the father's response are rendered in detail: "Her cries meant nothing to him" (59). This is a line taken almost verbatim from Hemingway's "Indian Camp," as Nick Adams's father performs a cesarean section on an Indian woman while his son watches. In another reference in description, the man in *The Road* remembers a time before the cataclysm, "a gray day in a foreign city" when "a cat at the corner turned and crossed the sidewalk and sat beneath a cafe awning," near where a lone woman sits at a table with "her head in her hands" (187). This memory of course recalls Hemingway's "Cat in the Rain." In *The Road* both style and allusion involve seemingly intentional, even playful allusions to the previous author's aesthetic of simplicity and his themes of human strife, isolation, and loss.

The novel is clearly the story of a father's powerful devotion to his son, and one of the most-common images encountered is the man holding the boy with desperate affection. But at least in the father's conception, the boy is from the onset an emanation of the divine. As the novel begins, this is stated clearly: "He knew only that the child was his warrant. He said: If he is not the word of God God never spoke" (5). Throughout the story, images of touching physical intimacy blend with the horrors of a lost world, as the man continually reassures his son that he is there to protect him, not only from physical threats but from his fears in waking consciousness and dreams. The man sees the boy not only as his son but also as a figure of divine import, and though the boy will display extraordinary qualities of kindness, the man's belief in the boy as the incarnate Word of God could be taken as an expression of mere sentiment, were it not for the many references to divinity, in the context of description and

allusions to God. Even as the novel takes a wasted creation as its setting, the divine if present is bound to the reality of human forms, identities, actions, and choices, and to the capacity to think and dream. Given the situation, however, the novel invites a number of questions: Are not human conceptions of the divine mere illusions? Doesn't the destructive and avaricious potential of the human race make plain the absence of a beneficent and active divinity? From the standpoint of literary interpretation and the reading of image patterns, should not the decimated world be read as a metaphor for a meaningless cosmological oblivion, the "heartless voids and immensities" Ishmael feared in *Moby-Dick*?

Further, if this materialist reading is valid, must not readers then take the essential message of the novel as consistent with that of many of the modern secular atheists? That is, meaning, purpose, and value cannot be found in the transcendent, however conceived, but instead they appear in the powerful but transitory experiences of connection and intimacy, from which a kind of happiness may be achieved. Without doubt the novel allows for this possibility. The hard reality of utter decimation and blight—in Melvillean terms—brings God himself to the bar of justice. But this notion depends much on a reading of the landscape as simple metaphor, the wasted land suggesting in rather basic terms a universal abyss. In addition, considering the mother in *The Road* and the suicidal atheist professor White in *The Sunset Limited* (works apparently written at nearly the same time), McCarthy's nonbelievers rarely speak from the perspective of hope, nor do they posit a universe where happiness is remotely possible. The mother's view of God is never articulated, but the depth of her despair is painfully clear: "I don't dream at all. . . . I am done with my own whorish heart and I have been

for a long time. You talk about taking a stand but there is no stand to take. . . . As for me my only hope is for eternal nothingness and I hope it with all my heart" (57).

The woman's emotional state and the worldview that emerges from it are a reasonable response to the circumstances of her life, having given birth to her only child in the wake of an apocalypse that yields the potential, not only of death, but of torture and the inhuman horror of cannibalism. The man has taught her how to kill herself with a sharp stone, and they carry a gun with bullets, which they have agreed to use before they will be taken prisoner. The dialogue before the woman's suicide involves a telling parallel to the atheist logic of Ivan in *The Brothers Karamazov,* but it is even more similar to the interchange between White and Black in *The Sunset Limited.* In all three cases, certain characters who hold fast to notions of hope and possibility, embodied in the divine incarnate in the world, are rendered silent by the rhetorical force of the hopeless nonbeliever. The similarity of the woman's words to those of White in the penultimate scene of the play is remarkable: "I don't believe in God. Can you understand that? Look around you, man. Can't you see? The clamor and din of those in torment has to be the sound most pleasing to his ear. . . . Brotherhood? Eternal life? Good god, man. Show me a religion that prepares one for death. For nothingness. There's a church I might enter. Yours prepares one only for more life. For dreams and illusions and lies" (137).

Unlike Ivan in Dostoyevsky's novel, McCarthy's despairing nonbelievers express themselves with pathos and emotional intensity rather than with an intricate and impenetrable logic born of rational argument. Still, their words when blended with the reality of their circumstances not only force their listeners into silence, but they come at least close to convincing them. The

man's tortured reflections throughout the novel alternate between a sense that God is wholly absent and a passionate anger that the world is God's creation and thus His ordination and responsibility. He ponders their lives in rigidly materialist terms defined by suffering. They exist in the midst of "borrowed time and borrowed world and borrowed eyes with which to sorrow it" (130), as they travel in a landscape "barren, silent, godless" (4). But at other times, he rails against a God he sees as active and intimately complicit in their circumstances. After waking one morning, he kneels as if to pray, saying, "Are you there? . . . Will I see you at the last? Have you a neck by which to throttle you? Have you a heart? . . . Oh God, he whispered. Oh God" (11–12). The lament, full of anger and beseeching hope, is reminiscent of Job's lament in the Old Testament. Present in the heart of this near believer is a complex blend of emotions and thoughts, ambiguous and tense as they are experienced and expressed. In contrast to the tortured sense of possibility in characters who court belief, McCarthy's nonbelievers (in these later works) are despairing and suicidal. Though the novel takes no absolute position on the existence of God and the role of the divine, it expresses with some force the value of belief as an essential ingredient of hope, seen especially in the father's sense of the boy's divinity and in the child's blending of kindness with his assent to God's presence and goodness.

In this context, reading the landscape in *The Road* as simple metaphor appears rather incomplete and limiting, and the wasted world emerges rather as the typological wilderness of the Old and New Testaments, a realm of spiritual quest and striving where the fortitudes of the spirit are put to the test. The perennial conflict of the "bad" and the "good" becomes evident in the ethical tension between father and son, which is always mediated by

their devotion to each other. This takes place in the "wilderness" of a destruction, through an epic battle full of religious implications informed by their encounter with the ambiguous wanderer Ely, a man who claims the name while confessing it is not in fact his own. They meet the starving old man, and the boy beseeches his father to feed him from their scant stores. Against his impulse the father agrees, and as the two men talk late at night they ponder the divine. In spite of his doubts, the man sees the boy as more than blood and sinew. Ely and the father have been painfully considering the nature of death, and the father speculates that God is aware of each distinct human destiny. Ely responds with a playful paradox: "There is no God and we are his prophets" (170). But the father's commitment to the son transcends impulse and instinct, and he asks: "What if I said that he's a god?" (172). Ely reacts in a similar way to the woman, saying, "I'm past all that now. . . . Where men can't live gods fare no better. . . . It's better to be alone . . . to be on the road with the last god would be a terrible thing" (172). The old man is bereft of faith and craves his own death, encouraging the man to join him in his passive hope for oblivion. Given his name, his status as a wanderer, and his preoccupation with ultimate questions, he suggests the prophet figures of the Old Testament and, more particularly, in his playful denial of the divine he implies the figure of Satan, who tempts Christ in the wilderness. The landscape then is rife with richer and more-telling figurative associations, more than simple metaphor would suggest, reflecting a mature reflection on the nature of transcendent reality. In the end, though, God is imagined in unconventional terms, and the parallel to *The Sunset Limited* is again quite fascinating. As the father is dying, he comes to believe in the "goodness" that has always found them, referring to the boy's "luck." Knowing

that he is leaving the boy alone, he makes every effort to sustain their connection, telling his son that he will speak to him after he has died, and if the boy listens the father will respond. The son remembers, and his luck proves true when he is discovered and taken in by a group of survivors much like himself. A woman speaks to him of God and he tries to pray, but in the end his prayers resolve themselves in conversations with his father. The woman sees nothing irreverent or unsettling in this: "He tried to talk to God but the best thing was to talk to his father and he did talk to him and he didn't forget. The woman said that was all right. She said that the breath of God was his breath yet though it pass from man to man through all of time" (286). Emerging from this interchange are two possibilities. On the one hand, the divine in human conception may be a projection of the capacity for hope, and notions of the divine help to sustain intimacy even in death through memory and imagination. But on the other hand, from the woman's point of view, God is immanent in the breath of the living and continues, perpetuating itself through the bonds of human connection, in the interior emotional forces that bind those relationships. This is essentially the perspective of the street preacher Black in *The Sunset Limited,* who claims Christ's real presence in acts of benevolence and self-sacrifice. More broadly, it reflects a form of Existential Christianity rooted in Søren Kierkegaard, Paul Tillich, Rudolph Bultmann, and John Macquarrie, and is expressed artistically in the works of Fyodor Dostoyevsky. This theology finds God in the embodied reality of the material world, in a father and son and the stubborn will that binds them, as well as in a family that rescues a child who is not their own.[15] It is a concept of the divine that is largely contiguous with the "panentheist" perspective found in many previous works, particularly in *Suttree.* This

metaphysics and guarded religiosity is mature and unflinching, devoid of sentimental conceptions of God, the world, and the hard realities that define them, since "all things of grace and beauty such as one holds them to one's heart have a common provenance in pain" (54). Even the blessings conferred—the heartfelt love of the man and the boy, the hope of a world renewed—are imbued with a tortured sense of brevity and loss.

These profound questions present themselves to the characters in the same way they have throughout human history, becoming more pressing in times of crisis. But in the end they remain unanswerable in objective terms. Many of the truths people live by must be constituted at a deeper psychological level and are born of experience and reflection—and perhaps from a capacity to imagine that may derive from more mysterious realms of phenomenal reality, which transcend scientific inquiry and the probing empirical intellect of the Enlightenment. At the heart of this are the complexities of human consciousness. Early in the novel, the father warns the son:

> Just remember that the things you put into your head are there forever. . . . You might want to think about that.
>
> You forget some things, don't you?
>
> Yes. You forget what you want to remember and you remember what you want to forget. (12)

This psychological insight foreshadows the father's more direct admonition that the boy take hold of his dreams, since dreams of hope and possibility suggest resignation and acceptance of death, and nightmares and fear are evidence of the survival instinct. Both notions are debatable but full of potential wisdom, as they imply the immense and paradoxical density of the human consciousness as its stands within and against a universe that is

beyond knowing. In the end *The Road* is set within an imagined but wholly plausible human history, emerging as a parable of human striving that takes form in the journey of a father and son, perhaps becoming again the "one tale" articulated by the travelers in *The Crossing.* As they traverse the narrative pathway of that storied journey, they are "carrying the fire," an evocative image prefigured clearly in the epilogue of *Blood Meridian* and in the final monologue in *No Country for Old Men,* reflecting perhaps the unorthodox mysticism of Jakob Böhme. But the image finds its origins earlier in the light of the campfire, when Culla Holme pleads for the life of the child he has abandoned. It even appears by implication in the formless "voice" in *Blood Meridian,* which binds the hard reality of the physical world into mysterious unity. For all McCarthy's interest in the possibilities of language, perhaps in the mystical content of the Word made Flesh in the figure of the boy, *The Road* ends in silence, with a description of a time before words: "In the deep glens where . . . all things were older than man and they hummed of mystery" (287). Darkness, desolation, isolation, the brute reality of an indifferent world: these are the patterns of experience Cormac McCarthy forces upon those who choose to read him. They remain present in *The Road,* balanced more intricately with aspects of experience found as early as *The Orchard Keeper.* They involve the interrelationship of life and land, the force of imagination, as well as the redemptive power of community and human intimacy—all in a world that yields its heart only in fleeting moments—of horror, yes, and metaphysical dread, but blended and imbued with inexpressible beauty.

Notes

All parenthetical citations in the body of this book refer to the readily available Vintage Books paperback editions of McCarthy's works.

Chapter 1—Understanding Cormac McCarthy

1. Josyph, "Tragic Ecstasy: A Conversation [with Harold Bloom] about Cormac McCarthy's *Blood Meridian*," 208.

2. Richard B. Woodward, "McCarthy's Venomous Fiction," 5.

3. Robert Coles, "The Stranger," *New Yorker,* 26 August 1974, 87–90.

4. The first extensive book-length study of McCarthy's works is Vereen M. Bell's 1988 *The Achievement of Cormac McCarthy*. Bell claims that the novels through *Blood Meridian* are characterized by an "ambiguous nihilism" in which both characters and the world function within a meaningless and amoral void. This study was published before the Border Trilogy and the later novels and plays, in which one finds a softening of perspective. But in "Naming, Knowing and Nothingness," Arnold argues that even the early novels involve a "moral gauge" that suggests systems of value and notably religious sensibilities, however obscurely articulated.

5. Woodward, "McCarthy's Venomous Fiction," 4.

6. For an interesting and useful distinction between potential permutations of the southern gothic, see Palmer, "Southern Gothic and Appalachian Gothic."

7. This statement appears in Tennessee Williams's "Introduction to Carson McCullers: Reflections in a Golden Eye," collected in *Where I Live: Selected Essays of Tennessee Williams* (New York: New Directions, 1978), 42.

Chapter 2—The Southern Works

1. See Edwin T. Arnold, "*The Stonemason:* The Unmaking of a Play."

2. Granville Hicks, "Six Firsts of Summer," *Saturday Review,* 12 June 1965, 35.

3. Gabriel Chevallier, *Kirkus Reviews,* 1 March 1965, 271.

4. Katherine Gauss Jackson, "Books in Brief," *Harper's,* July 1965, 112.

5. Anon., "Americans in Debt," *Times Literary Supplement,* 10 March 1966, 185.

6. James R. Frakes, "Juicy Fruit," *New York Herald Tribune Book Week,* 4 July 1965, 14.

7. For a thorough treatment of these historical tensions, see Ragan, "Values and Structure in *The Orchard Keeper.*"

8. See Richard Slotkin's *Regeneration Through Violence: The Mythology of the American Frontier, 1600 to 1860* (Middleton, Conn.: Wesleyan University Press, 1973), 4.

9. See David Paul Ragan's "Values and Structure in *The Orchard Keeper.*"

10. Thomas Lask, "Southern Gothic," *New York Times,* 23 September 1968, 33.

11. Robert Coles, "The Empty Road," *New Yorker,* 22 March 1969, 137.

12. Ibid.

13. Guy Davenport, "Appalachian Gothic," *New York Times Book Review,* 29 September 1968, 7.

14. André Deutsch, "Wandering the Warrens," *Times Literary Supplement,* 4 December 1970, 1409.

15. Patrick Cruttwell, "Plumbless Recrements," *Washington Post Book World,* 24 November 1968, 18.

16. Ibid.

17. See Arnold, "Naming, Knowing, and Nothingness: McCarthy's Moral Parables."

18. Coles, "The Empty Road," 137.

19. Herman Melville, "Hawthorne and His Mosses," in *Moby-Dick,* edited by Hershel Parker and Harrison Hayford, 2nd ed., 517–32 (New York: Norton, 2002).

20. Anon., "Depraved," *Atlantic Monthly,* May 1974, 128.

21. This potential link to film sources is first noted and explored by Dianne C. Luce in *Reading the World: Cormac McCarthy's Tennessee Period.*

22. Anon., "Depraved," 128.

23. Peter S. Prescott, "Dangerous Witness," *Newsweek,* 7 January 1974, 63–67.

24. Richard P. Brickner, "A Hero Cast Out, Even by Tragedy," *New York Times Book Review,* 13 January 1974, 6–7.

25. Robert Coles, "The Stranger," 87–90.

26. Ibid.

27. Doris Grumbach, "Practitioner of Ghastliness," *New Republic,* 9 February 1974, 26–28.

28. Ibid.

29. Roy Foster, "Downhill-billy," *Times Literary Supplement,* 25 April 1975, 445.

30. Jerome Charyn, "Doomed Huck," *New York Times Book Review,* 18 February 1979, 7:14–15.

31. Edward Rothstein, "A Homologue of Hell on a River of Death," *Washington Post,* 19 March 1979, B2.

32. Ibid.

33. Geoffrey Wolff, "Deadbeats, Live Wires: Hanging Out with McCarthy," *Esquire,* March 1979, 80.

34. Walter Sullivan, "Model Citizens and Marginal Cases: Heroes of the Day," *Sewanee Review* 87 (April 1979): 342.

35. Ibid.

36. Sandra Salmans, "Down and out in Knoxville," *Times Literary Supplement,* 2 May 1980, 500.

37. Anatole Broyard, "Where All Tales Are Tall," *New York Times,* 20 January 1979, 19.

38. For a detailed consideration of the carnivalesque in *Suttree,* see Canfield, "The Dawning of the Age of Aquarius"

39. T. S. Eliot, "The Waste Land," *The Complete Poems and Plays: 1909–1950* (New York: Harcourt, Brace, 1952), 43.

Chapter 3—Into the West

1. For a thorough consideration of Judge Holden as a Eurocentric Enlightenment figure, see Monk, "'An Impulse to Action, and Undefined Want.'"

2. Walter Sullivan, "About Any Kind of Meanness You Can Name," *Sewanee Review* 93 (Fall 1985): 652.

3. Ibid.

4. Ibid.

5. Caryn James, "Is Everybody Dead Around Here?," *New York Times Book Review,* 28 April 1985, 31.

6. Andrew Hislop, "The Wild Bunch," *Times Literary Supplement,* 21–27 April 1989, 436.

7. Edwin Arnold, review of *Blood Meridian, Appalachian Journal* 13 (Fall 1985): 103–4. For a discussion of the novel as an exploration of the darkest manifestations of American conquest, see Douglas, "The Flawed Design."

8. Richard Slotkin, *Gunfighter Nation: The Myth of the Frontier in Twentieth-Century America* (New York: Harper Perennial, 1992), 628.

9. Gnostic cosmology and mythology in the novel have been explored in detail by Daugherty in "Gravers False and True" and Wallach in "Judge Holden." See also Woodson, "'The Lighted Display Case.'"

10. Harold Bloom notes the parallel to Milton's *Lycidas* in "Tragic Ecstasy," his interview with Peter Josyph. In this interview Bloom treats the epilogue, which includes his Promethean reading. In "Walter De Maria's Lightning Field and McCarthy's Enigmatic Epilogue," Campbell explores in detail De Maria's work as a potential historical source for the image itself.

11. In "McCarthy and the Sacred," Arnold explores the implications of Böhme's conceptions in a reading of the second novel of the Border Trilogy.

Chapter 4—The Border Trilogy

1. For a consideration of the cold war contest in the Border Trilogy, see Hawkins, "Cold War Cowboys and the Culture of Nostalgia." In "Right and False Suns," Hunt explores the second novel in the trilogy in the context of the cold war.

2. See Arnold, "The Last of the Trilogy: First Thoughts on *Cities of the Plain.*"

3. The film adaptation of *All the Pretty Horses,* starring Matt Damon and Penélope Cruz, received mixed though generally negative reviews, the consensus being that the storyline was truncated and the characters were not sufficiently developed. Subsequent to the film's release, information emerged that the running time of Thornton's original version was between three and four hours, and that at least an hour was excised from the original by producer/distributor Harvey Weinstein. Some attempts have been made to release a director's cut on DVD, but arrangements cannot be completed with Daniel Lanois, the composer of the original score. In the version edited under the authority of Weinstein, Lanois's score was replaced by another composed by Marty Stuart. Apparently for this reason, there are no current plans to release a director's cut that includes Thornton's more complete adaptation of the novel.

4. Anon., review of *All the Pretty Horses, New Yorker,* 10 August 1992, 79.

5. Madison Smartt Bell, "The Man Who Understood Horses," *New York Times Book Review,* 17 May 1992, 9, 11.

6. Christopher Zenowich, "Coming of Age: A Lyrical Tale of the Southwest from Cormac McCarthy," *Chicago Tribune,* 10 May 1992, 14: 5, 10.

7. There is little certainty about McCarthy's current reading practice, and he has claimed in recent years to prefer nonfiction to fiction. But he has attested to a genuine affinity for the film version of *Lonesome Dove,* which was a very comprehensive and effective film adaptation, winning an Emmy award in 1988.

8. John Sutherland, "Adventures over the Rio Grande," *Times Literary Supplement,* 2 April 1993, 21.

9. Ibid.

10. Douglas Cooper, letter to the editor, *Times Literary Supplement,* 30 April 1993, 15.

11. Daniel Conaway, letter to the editor, *Times Literary Supplement,* 30 April 1993, 15.

12. Michael Coffey, "New Grit: The Dawn of the McCarthy Era," *Village Voice,* 19 May 1992, 70.

13. For a detailed treatment of the dream motif in the Border Trilogy in general, see Arnold, "'Go to Sleep.'" See also Wallach, "Theater, Ritual, and Dream in the Border Trilogy."

14. In "'When You Wake,'" Luce explores the varied complexities of John Grady Cole as mythic hero.

15. This image is prefigured in *Blood Meridian* as Judge Holden stands behind the figure of the coiner, evoking the Gnostic demiurge.

16. When McCarthy became a fellow at the Santa Fe Institute, he was exposed to a variety of sometimes radical ideas in the physical sciences, including "chaos theory." This theory of mathematical causality is best understood by the metaphor of the "butterfly effect," the idea that a butterfly flapping its wings in one part of the world causes a typhoon in another. The implication here is that within closed physical systems extremely small changes have radical and unpredictable effects. It is unknown whether McCarthy encountered these ideas before he wrote *All the Pretty Horses,* and *No Country for Old Men* deals more directly with them through the more extended metaphor of the coin toss. But he certainly anticipates something similar to chaos theory in this first novel of the Border Trilogy, as well as in the ambiguous coiner in *Blood Meridian.*

17. Sven Birkerts, "The Lone Soul State," *New Republic,* 11 July 1994, 38–41.

18. Robert Hass, "Travels with a She-Wolf," *New York Times Book Review,* 12 June 1994, 1, 39–40.

19. Gail Caldwell, "Dark Country in 'The Crossing,'" *Boston Globe,* 19 June 1994, B23, 25.

20. Ibid.

21. Michael Wood, review of *The Crossing, London Review of Books,* 6 October 1994, 18.

22. In "Fenimore Cooper's Literary Offenses" (1895), Mark Twain satirizes Cooper for the implausible characters and plot devices in the *Leatherstocking Tales*. This essay has emerged as one of the most important statements of American realism. In spite of it, elements of the romance tradition are evident in *Adventures of Huckleberry Finn*.

23. These terms are drawn from E. M. Forster's *Aspects of the Novel* (1927), round characters reflecting psychological complexity and dynamic characters manifesting observable and significant change.

24. Two valuable explorations of the wolf as a figure are McBride, "*The Crossing's* Noble Savagery," and Robisch, "The Trapper Mystic."

25. There is an intertextual quality to this sequence, recalling the Bundren family's journey to bury their wife and mother, Addie, in William Faulkner's *As I Lay Dying* and Woodrow Call's heroic act of returning the body of his friend Augustus McCrae in Larry McMurty's *Lonesome Dove*.

26. Details of McCarthy's life are notoriously difficult to document, particularly as they related to his eclectic reading practice. In "The Road as Matrix," Luce writes, "McCarthy was thinking about the role of narrative in our lives and had done some reading in Hegel that seems to have influenced his ideas at least by Fall 1991" (202). Luce provides a thorough treatment of the various tales and their relationship.

27. Herman Melville, *Moby-Dick* (1851; New York: Norton, 2002), 345.

28. For an exploration of the structure of the stories as they appear in the novel, specifically as they reflect James Moffett's *Teaching the Universe of Discourse,* see Gilbert, "Discourse Theory in *The Crossing*." For a thorough treatment of theatrical techniques in the novel, see Wallach, "Theatre, Ritual, and Dream in the Border Trilogy."

29. See James Keegan, "'Save Yourself."

30. In "Horses, Houses, and the Gravy to Win," Jay Ellis and Natalka Palczynski discuss Billy Parham as both knight and squire, as well as the desire for domesticity in the major characters of the Border Trilogy.

31. See Arnold, "Naming, Knowing, and Nothingness." See also Snyder, "Cowboy Codes in Cormac McCarthy's the Border Trilogy."

32. For a comprehensive treatment of the use of dreams in the Border Trilogy, see Arnold, "'Go to Sleep.'"

33. Sara Mosle, "Don't Let Your Babies Grow Up to Be Cowboys," *New York Times Book Review,* 17 May 1998, 16.

34. Ibid.

35. Ibid.,18.

36. Alan Cheuse, "Dark Quest," *Chicago Tribune,* 31 May 1998, 3.

37. Jay Ellis, review of *Cities of the Plain, Concho River Review* 12 (Fall 1998): 83.

38. Paul Quinn, "Crossing the Mountains of Mexico," *Times Literary Supplement,* 19 June 1998, 3.

39. Cheuse, "Dark Quest," 3.

Chapter 5—The Later Works

1. "Whales and Men" has never been produced or published. A copy is in the Cormac McCarthy papers housed in the Southwestern Writers' Collection of the Albert B. Alkek Library at Southwest Texas State University in San Marcos.

2. *The Sunset Limited* was first performed in the Steppenwolf Theater in Chicago, and later in New York and Galway, Ireland.

3. The novel began as a screenplay in 1984. However, available evidence suggests the Coen Brother's adaptation did not use McCarthy's screenplay in any substantial way but worked primarily from the novel.

4. Walter Kirn, *New York Times Book Review,* 24 July 2005, 9.

5. Ibid.

6. McCarthy himself expressed a general satisfaction with the adaptation, as is made clear by his willingness to be interviewed with the Coen brothers in *Vanity Fair* after the film's release. Critical consensus on the film's merits seems widespread and well deserved. Though omission of some elements of the novel's material is necessary in any feature-length film adaptation, it is important to note that Ed Tom Bell's voiceover in the film omits the frequent references to his wife, Loretta, and her role (played in two brief cameos by Tess Harper) is extremely limited. Also omitted is his war confession to Uncle Ellis as well as Ellis's comment about the limited role of God in the world.

7. Richard B. Woodward, "McCarthy's Venomous Fiction," *New York Times,* 19 April 1992, 4.

8. Though written before *No Country for Old Men,* Gordon E. Slethaug's *Beautiful Chaos: Chaos Theory and Metachaotics in Recent American Fiction* deals with the idea in McCarthy's earlier works.

9. Janet Maslin, "The Road Through Hell: Paved with Desperation," *New York Times,* 25 September 2006, 1.

10. William Kennedy, "Left Behind," *New York Times Book Review,* 8 October 2006, 11.

11. Ibid., 10.

12. Ibid., 11.

13. Philip Connors, "Crenellated Heat," *London Review of Books,* 25 January 2007, 15.

14. Ibid.

15. For a detailed consideration of Existential Christianity in the Border Trilogy, particularly as it relates to the ideas of Martin Heidegger, see Canfield, "Crossing from the Wasteland into the Exotic in McCarthy's Border Trilogy."

Selected Bibliography

Works by Cormac McCarthy

Novels

The Orchard Keeper. New York: Random House, 1965.
Outer Dark. New York: Random House, 1968.
Child of God. New York: Random House, 1974.
Suttree. New York: Random House, 1979.
Blood Meridian; or, The Evening Redness in the West. New York: Random House, 1985.
All the Pretty Horses. New York: Knopf, 1992.
The Crossing. New York: Knopf, 1994.
Cities of the Plain. New York: Knopf, 1998.
No Country for Old Men. New York: Knopf, 2005.
The Road. New York: Knopf, 2006.

Published Plays and Screenplays

The Stonemason: A Play in Five Acts. Hopewell, N.J.: Ecco Press, 1994.
The Gardener's Son: A Screenplay. Hopewell, N.J.: Ecco Press, 1996.
The Sunset Limited: A Novel in Dramatic Form. New York: Vintage, 2006.

Unpublished Screenplays

"Whales and Men" (n.d.). Manuscript held in the Southwestern Writers' Collection, Albert B. Alkek Library, Texas State University.
"Cities of the Plain" (1984). Manuscript held in the Southwestern Writers' Collection, Albert B. Alkek Library, Texas State University.
"No Country for Old Men" (n.d., but began as a screenplay in 1984).

Uncollected Short Fiction

"Wake for Susan." *Phoenix* (University of Tennessee at Knoxville), 1959.
"A Drowning Incident." *Phoenix,* 1960.

Interviews

Woodward, Richard B. "McCarthy's Venomous Fiction." *New York Times Magazine,* 19 April 1992, 28–31.

———. "Cormac McCarthy; Cormac McCarthy Would Rather Hang Out With Physicists Than with Writers." *Vanity Fair,* 1 August 2005.

Kushner, David. "Cormac McCarthy's Apocalypse." *Rolling Stone,* 27 December 2008.

Works about Cormac McCarthy

Books

Bell, James Luther. *Cormac McCarthy's West: The Border Trilogy Annotations.* El Paso: Texas Western Press, 2002.

Bell, Vereen M. *The Achievement of Cormac McCarthy.* Baton Rouge: Louisiana State University Press, 1988.

Bloom, Harold. *Modern Critical Views: Cormac McCarthy.* Philadelphia: Chelsea, 2002.

Bowers, James. *Reading Cormac McCarthy's Blood Meridian.* Boise State University Western Writers Series 139. Boise, Idaho: Boise State University, 1999.

Cant, John. *Cormac McCarthy and the Myth of American Exceptionalism.* New York: Routledge, 2007.

Ellis, Jay. *No Place for Home: Spatial Constraint and Character Flight in the Novels of Cormac McCarthy.* New York: Routledge, 2006.

Guillemin, Georg. *The Pastoral Vision of Cormac McCarthy.* College Station: Texas A&M University Press, 2004.

Holloway, David. *The Late Modernism of Cormac McCarthy.* Westport, Conn.: Greenwood, 2002.

Jarrett, Robert L. *Cormac McCarthy.* New York: Twayne, 1997.

Luce, Dianne C. *Reading the World: Cormac McCarthy's Tennessee Period.* Columbia: University of South Carolina Press, 2009.

Owens, Barkley. *Cormac McCarthy's Western Novels.* Tucson: University of Arizona Press, 2000.

Sepich, John. *Notes on Blood Meridian.* Louisville: Bellarmine College Press, 1993.

Tatum, Stephen. *Cormac McCarthy's All the Pretty Horses: A Reader's Guide.* New York: Continuum, 2002.

Journal

Cormac McCarthy Journal (Cormac McCarthy Society).

Essay Collections

Arnold, Edwin T., and Dianne C. Luce, eds. *A Cormac McCarthy Companion: The Border Trilogy.* Jackson: University Press of Mississippi, 2001.

———, eds. *Perspectives on Cormac McCarthy.* Rev. ed. Jackson: University Press of Mississippi, 1999.

Chollier, Christine, ed. *Cormac McCarthy: Uncharted Territories / Territoires Inconnus.* Reims: Presses Universitaires de Reims, 2003.

Hall, Wade, and Rick Wallach, eds. *Sacred Violence.* Vol. 1, *A Reader's Companion to Cormac McCarthy.* El Paso: Texas Western Press, 1995.

———, eds. *Sacred Violence.* Vol. 2, *Cormac McCarthy's Western Novels.* El Paso: Texas Western Press, 2002.

Lilley, James D., ed. *Cormac McCarthy: New Directions.* Albuquerque: University of New Mexico Press, 2002.

Wallach, Rick, ed. *Myth, Legend, Dust: Critical Responses to Cormac McCarthy.* Manchester: Manchester University Press, 2001.

Selected Articles and Essays

Ambrosiano, Jason. "Blood in the Tracks: Catholic Postmodernism in *The Crossing.*" *Southwestern American Literature* 25 (Fall 1999): 83–91.

Arnold, Edwin T. "'Go to Sleep': Dreams and Visions in the Border Trilogy." In Arnold and Luce, eds., *A Cormac McCarthy Companion,* 37–72.

————. "The Last of the Trilogy: First Thoughts on *Cities of the Plain.*" In Arnold and Luce, eds., *Perspectives on Cormac McCarthy,* 221–47.

————. "McCarthy and the Sacred: A Reading of *The Crossing.*" In Lilley, ed., *Cormac McCarthy,* 215–38.

————. "The Mosaic of McCarthy's Fiction, Continued." In Hall and Wallach, eds., *Sacred Violence,* 2:179–87.

————. "Naming, Knowing, and Nothingness: McCarthy's Moral Parables." In Arnold and Luce, eds., *Perspectives on Cormac McCarthy,* 45–69.

————. "*The Stonemason:* The Unmaking of a Play." *Southern Quarterly* 33 (Winter/Spring 1995): 117–29.

Campbell, Christopher D. "Walter De Maria's Lightning Field and McCarthy's Enigmatic Epilogue: Y que clase de lugar es este?" *Cormac McCarthy Journal* 2 (Spring 2002): 40–55.

Canfield, Douglas J. "Crossing from the Wasteland into the Exotic in McCarthy's Border Trilogy." In Arnold and Luce, eds., *A Cormac McCarthy Companion,* 256–69.

————. "The Dawning of the Age of Aquarius: Abjection, Identity, and the Carnivalesque in Cormac McCarthy's *Suttree.*" *Contemporary Literature* 44 (Winter 2003): 664–96.

Daugherty, Leo. "Gravers False and True: *Blood Meridian* as Gnostic Tragedy." In Arnold and Luce, eds., *Perspectives on Cormac McCarthy,* 159–74.

Douglas, Christopher. "The Flawed Design: American Imperialism in N. Scott Momaday's *House Made of Dawn* and Cormac McCarthy's *Blood Meridian.*" *Critique* 45 (Fall 2003): 3–24.

Ellis, Jay, and Natalka Palczynski. "Horses, Houses, and the Gravy to Win: Chivalric and Domestic Roles in the Border Trilogy." In Hall and Wallach, eds., *Sacred Violence,* 2:105–25.

Frye, Steven. "Cormac McCarthy's 'world in its making': Romantic Naturalism in *The Crossing.*" *Studies in American Naturalism* 2 (Summer 2007): 46–65.

————. "Fate Without Foreknowledge: Style and Image in the Late Naturalism of *Suttree.*" *Cormac McCarthy Journal* 4 (Spring 2005): 184–94.

———. "Wilderness Typology, American Scripture, and the Interpreter's Eye: The Interior Landscapes of McCarthy's Western Novels." In Chollier, ed., *Cormac McCarthy,* 115–21.

Grammar, John M. "A Thing Against Which Time Will Not Prevail: Pastoral and History in Cormac McCarthy's South." In Arnold and Luce, eds., *Perspectives on Cormac McCarthy,* 29–44.

Hawkins, Susan. "Cold War Cowboys and the Culture of Nostalgia." In Chollier, ed., *Cormac McCarthy,* 95–103.

Hunt, Alexander. "Right and False Suns: Cormac McCarthy's *The Crossing* and the Advent of the Atomic Age." *Southwestern American Literature* 23 (Spring 1998): 31–37.

Josyph, Peter. "Tragic Ecstasy: A Conversation [with Harold Bloom] about McCarthy's *Blood Meridian.*" In Hall and Wallach, eds., *Sacred Violence,* 2:205–21.

Keegan, James. "'Save Yourself': The Boundaries of Theodicy and the Signs of *The Crossing.*" *Cormac McCarthy Journal* 1 (Spring 2001): 44–61.

Luce, Dianne C. "The Road as Matrix: The World as Tale in *The Crossing.*" In Arnold and Luce, eds., *Perspectives on Cormac McCarthy,* 195–219.

———. "The Vanishing World of Cormac McCarthy's Border Trilogy." In Arnold and Luce, eds., *A Cormac McCarthy Companion,* 161–97.

———. "'When You Wake': John Grady Cole's Heroism in *All the Pretty Horses.*" In Hall and Wallach, eds., *Sacred Violence,* 1:155–67.

McBride, Molly. "*The Crossing's* Noble Savagery: The Wolf, the Indian, and the Empire." In Hall and Wallach, eds., *Sacred Violence,* 2:71–82.

McMurtry, Kim. "'Some Improvident God': Metaphysical Explorations in McCarthy's Border Trilogy." In Hall and Wallach, eds., *Sacred Violence,* 2:143–57.

Monk, Nick. "'An Impulse to Action, and Undefined Want': Modernity, Flight, and Crisis in the Border Trilogy and *Blood Meridian.*" In Hall and Wallach, eds., *Sacred Violence,* 2:83–103.

Morrison, Gail Moore. "*All the Pretty Horses:* John Grady Cole's Expulsion from Paradise." In Arnold and Luce, eds., *Perspectives on Cormac McCarthy,* 175–94.

Palmer, Louis H., III. "Southern Gothic and Appalachian Gothic: A Comparative Look at Flannery O'Connor and Cormac McCarthy." *Journal of the Appalachian Studies Association* 3 (1991): 166–76

Peebles, Stacey. "What Happens to Country: The World to Come in Cormac McCarthy's Border Trilogy." In Hall and Wallach, eds., *Sacred Violence,* 2:127–42.

———. "Yuman Belief Systems and Cormac McCarthy's *Blood Meridian.*" *Texas Studies in Literature and Language* 45 (Summer 2003): 231–44.

Prather, William. "Absurd Reasoning in an Existential World: A Consideration of Cormac McCarthy's *Suttree.*" In Hall and Wallach, eds., *Sacred Violence,* 1:103–14.

Ragan, David Paul. "Values and Structure in *The Orchard Keeper.*" In Arnold and Luce, eds., *Perspectives on Cormac McCarthy,* 17–27.

Robisch, S. K. "The Trapper Mystic: Werewolves in *The Crossing.*" *Southwestern American Literature* 25 (Fall 1999): 50–54.

Scoones, Jacqueline. "The World on Fire: Ethics and Evolution in Cormac McCarthy's the Border Trilogy." In Arnold and Luce, eds., *A Cormac McCarthy Companion,* 131–60.

Sepich, John Emil. "'What kind of Indians was them?': Some Historical Sources in Cormac McCarthy's *Blood Meridian.*" In Arnold and Luce, eds., *Perspectives on Cormac McCarthy,* 123–43.

Snyder, Phillip A. "Cowboy Codes in Cormac McCarthy's Border Trilogy." In Arnold and Luce, eds., *A Cormac McCarthy Companion,* 198–227.

Wallach, Rick. "Cormac McCarthy's Metaphors of Antiquity and Deep Time." In Chollier, ed., *Cormac McCarthy,* 105–13.

———. "Judge Holden, *Blood Meridian*'s Evil Archon." In Hall and Wallach, eds., *Sacred Violence,* 1:125–36.

———. "Theatre, Ritual, and Dream in the Border Trilogy." In Hall and Wallach, eds., *Sacred Violence,* 2:159–77.

Wegner, John. "'Mexico para los Mexicanos': Revolution, Mexico, and McCarthy's Border Trilogy." *Southwestern American Literature* 25 (Fall 1999): 67–73.

———. "'Wars and Rumors of Wars' in Cormac McCarthy's Border Trilogy." In Arnold and Luce, eds., *A Cormac McCarthy Companion,* 73–91.

Woodson, Linda Townley. "'The Lighted Display Case': A Nietzschean Reading of Cormac McCarthy's Border Fiction." *Southern Quarterly* 38 (Summer 2000): 48–60.

Index